The Education of a White Parent

Wrestling with Race and Opportunity in the Boston Public Schools

Susan Naimark

ISBN 978-1-937146-12-2

Cover design by Ekua Holmes
Author photograph by Javier Antonio Dunn

Some of the material in this book first appeared in
Rethinking Schools magazine, www.rethinkingschools.org.

To parents nationwide who send their children to our public schools and are willing to do whatever it takes to ensure that those schools work well for *all* children.

In order to get beyond racism, we must first take account of race. There is no other way.

—Supreme Court Justice Harry Blackmun

The world of U.S. education is race dilemmas all the way "down." …Both our talk and our silence about race have real ramifications for what we do and do not do about racial inequality.

—Mica Pollock, editor of *Everyday Antiracism: Getting Real about Race in School*

Contents

Acknowledgments

When I first started writing about my school organizing experience, I had no idea where I was headed. I want to thank my first writing group at the Cambridge Center for Adult Education, whose members set me on the right path by stating loud and clear that my personal story was much more engaging than my proselytizing.

The Jamaica Plain Writers Group then patiently gave me feedback, chapter by chapter, year after year. Special thanks to Todd Fry and members of the LeadBoston class of 2007 for their early feedback and encouragement. Other valuable input, insights, and inspiration were provided by Kenneth Bailey, Barbara Beckwith, Michele Brooks, Kathy Brown, Gina Chirichigno, Chuck Collins, Amit Desai, Meck Groot, Sherry Grossman, Curdina Hill, David Hunt, Debby Irving, Lori Lobenstine, Paul Marcus, Rebecca Martin, Peggy McIntosh, Karla Nicholson, Susan O'Brien, Myrna Morales, Katy Schramm, Klare Shaw, Libbie Shufro, Bob Tumposky, and Boston's own Grub Street creative writing center. My first editor, Kate Victory Hannisian, helped shape my manuscript into a book. Beth Wallace then escorted the next draft through to its final form, asking hard questions and providing wise guidance on how to convey with clarity and strength the things that mattered most.

I want to thank my parents, posthumously, for teaching me the importance of speaking up when things don't seem right, and giving me some of the skills to do so. From them I learned the value of community, the need for collective effort, and the importance of integrity to sleeping well at night.

I never could have grown in my understanding of educational inequities and organizing, racism, the unearned benefits that come to me as a white person, and the complicated intersection of these topics without the patient support and friendship of hundreds of people who have travelled these roads ahead of me. Some are included in this book; many more are not. If our paths have crossed, you know who you are. And I thank you with deep gratitude and appreciation.

Lastly, the biggest thank you goes to my husband, John, and to my two sons, Ben and Jesse, who put up with my chronic absenteeism from family life for the better part of two decades. I can now say with great relief that we all came through fine, a testament to the strength of love, honesty, commitment, compassion—and a good dose of luck.

Introduction

"I THINK I'M LOST."

My brother David was calling me from a phone booth in Roxbury. This was the fall of 1975—way before cell phones. It was almost eleven at night. I had been expecting his arrival at my apartment for more than an hour.

I knew exactly where he was: at the gas station with the only pay phone along a desolate strip of Columbus Avenue, where all the houses had been torn down a decade earlier for a highway that was never built. For a mile in either direction, the number 49 bus route went past vacant lots filled with elbow-high weeds, trash, abandoned cars, and illegally dumped construction debris. That gas station would have been the first sign of life in the dark after David realized he missed my bus stop, which was now a mile behind him.

"OK, David, you went a little too far. Stay at the gas station where there's good lighting until you see the bus coming in the other direction."

You don't know how scared you should be right now. You need to get yourself the hell out of there as quickly as possible. I kept these thoughts to myself, not wanting to alarm my younger brother.

The mile-long stretch between that gas station in Roxbury and my home back in Boston's South End could just as well have been the no-man's-land of an international border crossing. This was the beginning of the second year of court-ordered desegregation of the Boston Public Schools. Roxbury was the heart of Boston's black community. White families were refusing to send their children to school in Roxbury, in defiance of the desegregation order. The racial tension throughout the city was off the charts.

This was not a good time for my brother—white, eighteen years old, and just arriving on his first trip to Boston from the quiet midwestern suburb where we grew up—to get inadvertently caught on the other side of the racial divide. Young black men his age had been beaten up at historically white Carson Beach on the other side of town, the assaults reported in the newspaper throughout the summer. David had no idea what he was walking into, and I worried about retaliation against an unsuspecting young white man. David had unknowingly traveled way outside of *my* comfort zone, and at that moment I was scared for his life.

Only a year earlier, white residents had stoned yellow school buses full of black children as they rolled across the city. Black parents had instructed their five-year-old children to keep their heads below the school bus windows to avoid being hit by rocks and broken glass on their way to and from school. Local and state police had been called in to line the streets of South Boston and ensure safe passage of the school buses. Violent outbursts had been a daily occurrence at Charlestown, East Boston, and South Boston High Schools. Large, angry groups of residents expressed their opposition to the racial integration of their neighborhood schools in no uncertain terms in these three white, working-class neighborhoods. The police presence barely kept the lid on the physical violence. It could not protect the students or their families from the emotional damage of those terrifying times.

I moved to Boston in January 1975, five months into the first school year of court-ordered desegregation. By then the violence had settled into a low simmer. Outbursts were less frequent but continued to erupt unpredictably across the city. I knew it was wrong that black people were being harassed and driven away from historically white parts of town, but I thought that was somebody else's problem. As a white twenty-year-old with no local family connections, I moved in a parallel universe, detached from the disruption that still engulfed much of the city.

I was too busy soaking in my first experience of big-city living. I reveled in leaving behind the dullness of my midwestern youth and launching my adult life on the East Coast. My great escape was complete when I found a place to live in one of the only racially integrated neighborhoods of Boston. In 1975, that was the main thing I cared about. Joni Mitchell's "Night in the City" played in a continuous loop through my brain every evening as I walked home from night school: "Night in the city looks pretty to me, night in the city looks fine..."

Only in retrospect can I appreciate the irony that I sought diversity in a city awash in racial violence and hatred. Despite my detachment, a voice inside me told me that the violence was *wrong*, as was the racial hatred that triggered it. My upbringing and my moral compass pointed the opposite direction of what I was seeing in the most entrenched white neighborhoods of Boston.

David arrived safely at my apartment that night, and I continued to move around town separated from the chaos, wearing on my jacket the symbol of support for desegregation: a red button bearing a single green branch sprouting multicolored leaves.

* * *

White resistance to court-ordered school desegregation in Boston in the mid-1970s defined the city's character for decades to come, and its imprint is still felt today. Thousands of white families pulled their children out of the public schools, sought refuge in Boston's extensive parochial school system, or moved out of the city. Politicians built careers on hatred or reconciliation, depending on which side of the battle lines they stood. The Boston School Committee, which had for over a decade ignored the appeals of black families for quality schools and equitable resources, became a national symbol of white opposition to racial equality.

Many books have been written about the desegregation of the Boston Public Schools. This is not one of them. Desegregation provides the context for my story, which began a decade later, when I enrolled my oldest child in the Boston Public Schools. By then, the earth had shifted under the city. The white population had declined from 525,000 in 1970 to 382,000 in 1980; the white student population of the public schools had plummeted from 61 percent to 35 percent. One of the most vocal opponents of school desegregation, South Boston's Ray Flynn, was elected mayor by a still overwhelmingly white electorate who viewed him as a hero for the stand he took. Black people learned to steer clear of whole neighborhoods and certain public beaches, and to be home by dark or risk their personal safety.

I held several jobs in communities of color during this period and did not find the racial hostility reciprocal. I heard many stories from co-workers of color about being told, "I'll sell you this sandwich, but you better get out of here quickly"—or worse—when stopping in a convenience store in a white neighborhood. I often waited at the bus stop after work, the only white person in sight, wondering why nobody bothered me. All I could think at the time was, *These people are much more gracious and forgiving than maybe they should be, given what they are up against in this city.*

Over the next three decades, I was to learn that the scars of desegregation ran deep throughout the city. I learned, too, that they looked very different, depending on where you were racially situated.

If someone had told me when I moved to Boston in 1975 that I was to become a member of the Boston School Committee two decades later, I would never have believed it—not in my wildest dreams—nor that I actually would *want* the position. And I hadn't a clue to my absolute naïveté about the forces of racism.

Half a lifetime later, here is my story of the unexpected life trajectory that took me from innocent young adult to concerned parent to activist to public official. I was stunned—no, outraged—by the racial inequities I found in the Boston Public Schools. Such inequities persist in public schools throughout the country, decades after the civil rights movement and desegregation orders. Many of the more blatant manifestations of racism have gone underground, but the effects remain as clear as ever: our schools continue to fail black and Latino students at alarming rates. I continue to be outraged that the wealthiest country in the world appears to be incapable of adequately educating all children. I believe what is missing is the political will and an understanding of the deeply entrenched impacts of our racial history. I hope that my story will help others understand and take action.

As a white, middle-class parent and city resident, I struggled with my role in addressing these problems. I slowly learned what that role could be as I raised my children, got involved in their schools, and stepped into leadership roles. I taught myself about the history of racial policies that led to current-day circumstances. I stumbled a lot. And I became convinced that we will never unravel the obstacles to our public schools working well for all children without addressing the legacy of racism.

One of my most difficult lessons was to understand that racism not only disadvantages people of color but *advantages* white people. I didn't have to do anything more than be born white to benefit from the present arrangements. As a result, my simply being a "good person" does not, by itself, correct the problem of racial inequities. Addressing racism demands a more active intervention. I have learned a variety of proactive roles for interrupting the deeply embedded patterns required to transform institutions. I don't always get it right. But I'm less afraid to try. In these pages, I share my wrestling with these issues in hopes of jumpstarting others on their own journey.

In 2012, as polarized national politics disintegrate into mutually assured destruction, the need for common ground is as great as ever. Public institutions that affirm shared values are the heart of a healthy democracy. Our public schools remain one of the few community institutions that have the potential to bring us together. They represent our dreams for our children and our collective future. As locally controlled institutions, they provide an opportunity to practice and, indeed, reclaim democracy.

I want this story to provide you with a glimmering of hope that these problems are not completely intractable. Pieces of the solutions can be found in many places—in schools and community groups and grassroots efforts in almost any city—and within ourselves.

At its root, the American problem of racism is of white people's making. As stated so well by the commission appointed by President Lyndon Johnson to determine the causes of race riots in the 1960s: "What white U.S. citizens never fully understand but what the Negro can never forget is that the white society is deeply implicated in the ghetto. White institutions created it, white institutions maintain it, and white society condones it." Sadly, these remarks remain as relevant in 2012 as they were four decades ago. Individual white people moving through twenty-first-century America did not create these institutions. Our white reaction, therefore, does not need to be about personal guilt. Yet, as white people, we have the luxury of looking the other way. This book is about the possibility of pursuing a different path, one of awareness and responsibility within a larger, multiracial, and multicultural society.

* * *

The stories in this book are as true as I can remember, yet memory can be a shifty thing. The public events included in this book are, to the best of my knowledge, chronologically and factually accurate. The timing of some of the personal interactions has been adjusted for the flow of the story. I have changed some names but used real names in the case of public figures and people who have had the opportunity to know what I wrote about them. Some of the details may differ from what others remember, but that is the nature of human memory.

A few words about language: One of the many challenges in writing a story about race is the question of naming people's racial identity. In a perfect world, race would not matter. But our world is far from that ideal. Race *does* matter—to the opportunities we are afforded, to our experiences as we move through life, and to our likelihood of success in virtually every aspect of American society: education, health, employment, wealth, and the list goes on. I have indicated the racial identity of key people whose roles were significant to this story. I have chosen not to identify everybody's race to avoid boring you, the reader, with a tedious level of detail.

In choosing terms of racial identity, I have used "black" primarily when referring to policies that use this identifier or when the people of color in my stories refer to themselves using this term. I use "African American" primarily when pointing out issues unique to the experience of black people who have lived in the United States for many generations, and when people in my stories refer to themselves using this term.

While the desegregation of the Boston Public Schools was, at the time, framed around black people and white people, the city's population has always been more diverse than this. The populations of other racial and ethnic groups have grown in size throughout the United States in the decades since the court-ordered desegregation of public schools across the country. I tend to focus more on the challenges unique to African Americans in acknowledgment of the deep legacy of slavery that continues to leave its marks on our country.

CHAPTER ONE

"They Need Whites There"

"SIGN HIM UP FOR THE KENNEDY SCHOOL. THEY NEED WHITES THERE."
The school secretary, a middle-aged white woman, barely looked up from the list of elementary schools spread on the counter between us. In my first interaction with the Boston Public Schools, I couldn't tell whether her statement was a suggestion or a directive. And I certainly couldn't fathom why she thought this piece of information would be a selling point to a parent registering a child to attend kindergarten in the fall.

In the decade since my brother's visit, I had transitioned from single to married, from South End to Jamaica Plain, from childless to the mother of two young sons. I thought I was prepared to entrust my first-born son to the still-turbulent Boston Public Schools. The school secretary's words seemed like an ominous start.

I was now living in a world far removed from my own childhood schooling, and I wasn't sure what to make of this first interaction with the Boston Public Schools.

My parents had decided to move out of Detroit in the early 1950s because of my mother's desire to be closer to the outlying lakes and woods. She had grown up in a small town with more space and fresh air than could be found around the brick bungalows of Detroit. As my parents zeroed in on the community that would became my childhood home, one of the largest real estate owners in the area pointedly told my father, "We don't sell to Jews here." My father threatened a lawsuit and bought property from another landowner.

My father protected his children from such stories at the time. I only learned this one when I probed as a young adult wanting to understand where my family fit into the narrative of white suburban flight. If the major property owners exercised such prejudice, it was no wonder that the community I grew up in was so racially homogenous.

One November morning when I was in first grade, two and a half decades before my son Ben would start kindergarten, Miss Barnett, our white teacher, gathered our all-white class in a cross-legged circle on the floor around the social studies bulletin board at the Franklin Village Elementary School. In a cheerfully neutral voice, Miss Barnett asked her six-year-old disciples who would vote for Nixon for president and who for Kennedy. I knew the right answer from overheard conversations at home. My hand proudly shot up for Kennedy. I slowly looked around, and a cloud of embarrassment formed in my brain as the realization dawned that I was alone in that camp.

Oh.

This newly awakened awareness of difference came into sharp focus by December, when the music teacher brought out Christmas carols and holiday concert practice began. My parents never commented on this that I can remember, but it was clearly not in our home repertoire. We dutifully lit candles for each of the eight nights of Hanukah, my mother explaining the story behind the holiday, of survival of the Jewish people against the destructive forces of the Syrian king over two thousand years earlier. Christmas was what other people did. My mother regularly reminded us that Hanukah was a minor holiday in the Jewish hierarchy.

I was horrified at the prospect of singing about the miracle of baby Jesus on stage in front of all those parents at my school. But I had no vocabulary to challenge the assumption of shared traditions that didn't match up with my strict Jewish upbringing. I silently mouthed the words, praying that *my* God wouldn't notice.

During my childhood, my encounters with people of color were limited to the African American cleaning women who came into some of the homes in our neighborhood. A few of my friends had live-in maids, who magically appeared every Monday and were delivered to the bus stop that returned them to their invisible families on Friday afternoons. At our house we had Gertrude, a heavy-set, dark-skinned, middle-aged African American woman who came to clean once a week.

Gertrude was unmarried and cared for a mentally retarded niece who lived with her. (In those days, we didn't use terms like "developmentally disabled.") My knowledge of Gertrude's life began and ended with those facts. Everything else about this woman who cleaned our bathrooms and mopped our kitchen floor once a week throughout my childhood remained a mystery.

My limited understanding of racial difference became further clouded one hot July night in 1967, when I was twelve years old. My family was driving home from a visit to my grandparents in northern New York State when the riots broke out in Detroit. Our usual route took us through Canada, then through the tunnel under the Detroit River and downtown Detroit to get home. We arrived at the U.S.-Canadian border that night to an unprecedented backup of traffic, slowly grinding to a stop behind a line of cars that stretched out of sight ahead of us. My father turned on the car radio. The usual rambunctiousness of four children and two adults packed tight for too many hours slipped out the window as we listened to the news. Stories about looting, street violence, and arson filled our now-silent car.

Customs agents were not letting most people through the tunnel. My father pulled up to the customs booth and was given the okay to proceed. As our family station wagon emerged from the tunnel into downtown Detroit, I shrank down in the dark corner of the back seat. Flames lit up the sky over the trees in the near distance. Sirens wailed. A column of army tanks rumbled past going the opposite direction on the expressway.

A war zone, I thought with horror. *We're driving through the next Civil War.*

By the time the riots subsided, dozens of people were dead, hundreds injured, thousands arrested, and five thousand left homeless. Thirteen hundred buildings had burnt to the ground. My family didn't talk about the reasons for the riots. All my twelve-year-old mind absorbed was that black people were mad and we needed to stay out of their way.

The following summer, I watched farmhouses torn down and fields torn up as suburbs sprang up all around us, as white flight took hold a seemingly safe twenty-miles distance from downtown Detroit. The surrounding communities for miles in every direction became a whirlwind of construction that lasted through my junior high school years. Looking

back, it's hard to believe that, at the time, I hadn't put together the relationship between the race riots of 1967 and the ensuing mad rush of white
families to create Detroit's farthest suburbs. The enduring image in my
mind was my friend Debby's old farmhouse, with a three-foot drop-off
carved into the dirt along the edge of her family's backyard, where the ex-
cavation for new houses began.

When I got my driver's license at sixteen, I began to take part in the
weekly ritual of driving Gertrude, the African American woman who
cleaned our house, to the bus that would take her home. Northland, the
shopping center that marked the demilitarized zone between city and suburbs, was the end of the line for city bus routes. I was curious about what
lay beyond, but the unspoken racial boundaries were well established. It
was as if we resided on different planets. And I thought that was just the
way things were. The Detroit riots of 1967 and the creation of whole new
suburbs out of hayfields and apple orchards had hardened the line between
city and suburb, black and white.

It wasn't until September 1971, when I was a senior, that the first student of color entered my high school. This created a stir of excitement and
novelty. Anticipating the start of school that year, one friend of mine said,
"And I can't wait to make friends with the new black boy!"

Even with my limited awareness of what this might feel like for the
school's first black student, the enthusiasm of my friend rubbed me the
wrong way. I had never heard of concepts like tokenism, but the image of
this young man being mobbed by new "friends" simply because of his skin
color left me uneasy. I graduated halfway through my senior year, leaving
in January with only an arm's-length observation of the largely uneventful
and nominal integration of my high school.

I moved to Boston three years later, enrolling in night school to study
architecture with a vague idea that it would allow me to do something creative related to rebuilding cities. After my first year of classes, my father,
who was a building contractor, remarked one day, "You know, any good architect I've ever worked with knows how to swing a hammer."

This sounded good to me; I was always quick to jump onto a new
challenge. I promptly signed up for a basic carpentry training course. My
future husband, John, was the instructor. He seemed nice enough. Shortly

after the course ended, one of the other students invited both of us on a group camping trip. By then, my attraction toward John had grown. In August 1977 we spent two weeks together in the wilderness, where the sparks flew between us. While John's New England Yankee upbringing was a stark contrast to my own background, he was just the right mix of gentle and firm, soft-spoken and committed to a vision of big-city living much like my own.

Trained as an architect, John was the only one of four sons to forgo the family business, which had been run by four generations of fruit juice makers. When we met, he was working for a nonprofit organization that rehabilitated vacant Jamaica Plain houses and sold them affordably to new owner-occupants. I was proud of the work he had chosen. I was also aware that his family viewed him as something of an outlier for it.

One month after the fated camping trip, I got an eviction notice from my South End landlord. The rental house I had been living in had been sold. I started looking for a studio apartment for myself.

"How'd you like to buy a vacant house in Jamaica Plain for $300?" John asked me one Saturday during a walk through the park.

He had just completed negotiations to buy the house for the nonprofit he worked for, only to learn that the city wouldn't allow the purchase. Public funds were needed to renovate the house, and the city deemed the costs too high to proceed.

The purchase price was right, and I responded with little hesitation. The house could be fixed up little by little.

"Sure!"

It was only after I accepted his offer that I realized he meant for us to buy the house *together*.

We pried the boards off a few windows with a crowbar to let in some light in order to move in on Halloween day 1977. The house had been abandoned when its longtime owner passed away a couple years earlier. The son who had inherited the house had written it off as an inner-city throwaway. All that was left by the time John and I arrived were dirty old overcoats strewn throughout the house, broken appliances in the burnt-out kitchen, a malfunctioning furnace, and holes in the kitchen and bathroom walls where the copper pipes had been.

I couldn't wait to create a home out of this mess. For no more than what would have been a rental deposit and first month's rent, John and I owned a barely livable, ten-room Victorian house. What more could a deeply in love and adventuresome twenty-three-year-old want in life?

As we began cleaning out knee-deep trash, a dozen neighborhood kids showed up to help. The six-unit apartment building next door was filled with Puerto Rican and Dominican families. The children invited us to their homes, where mothers and grandmothers offered home-cooked chicken and rice. The friendliness of our new neighbors reinforced my sense that this was a good move.

John's world unfolded to me like a foreign country, unlike anything I knew as a Midwest-raised Jew. When I was a teenager, my father had made me look up the word "iconoclast" in the dictionary one day when he used it to describe himself. John grew up in a Norman Rockwell world, where family members held hands every Thanksgiving around the dinner table and recited the Lord's Prayer—I imagine much the same as they had done since his mother's forebears came off the *Mayflower*.

My father and grandfather had been union organizers. John's father and grandfather before him ran a successful family business that kept its employees happy, with a clear aversion to any hint of union sentiment.

Most of my family vacations growing up were road trips to visit my mother's family in northern New York State. John's father and his family summered at the same cottage on a lake in New Hampshire from the time he first traveled there by train and milk wagon at age three until he passed away at ninety-seven.

I grew up in a world where summer was a noun, not a verb.

I was at once in awe of and repelled by the security that John's world offered. The house where John grew up was full of furniture that had been in the family for generations, a few pieces hand-carved by his great-grandfather. You could count on strawberry shortcake on the first Sunday in June at the church social hall, and John's mother scolding if the biscuit recipe was altered in the slightest. At every family birthday party and Mother's Day gathering, tradition placed me firmly in the kitchen of his parent's two-hundred-year-old farmhouse, washing and hand-drying the antique china. I bristled that the sole kitchen duty of the men in the family was to wander in and pick at the leftovers. My father was always proud to say that he married a feminist before anybody knew what that was.

I gradually became an accepted visitor at John's parents' home, allowed to enter but always reminded that I was, in the end, not one of them. It must have taken my mother-in-law fifteen years to stop asking me about the "Jewish Christmas."

Ouch. No matter how many times I tried to explain the origins of Hanukah, and that it was in fact a very minor holiday in the Jewish calendar, she kept coming back to the only analogy she could muster.

Despite these differences, John and I made a great team as we reglazed broken windows and laid out our new kitchen. Two years later, we married.

In 1981 I gave birth to Ben and, three years later, to his younger brother, Jesse. By then, the old wallpaper was long gone, and our house was *home.* John, like most of the men in his family, was comfortable and gentle with babies and young children. Unlike many of the men in his family, he agreeably changed and washed diapers, too. To me, this marriage seemed to be working out fine.

My dinnertime conversations with John soon veered toward schooling.

"We should start looking into the Boston Public Schools."

For me, there was no debate about whether to send our children to public schools. That was all I knew. Not only were private schools, including parochial schools, foreign territory to me—I had never set foot in either when it was time to send Ben off to kindergarten—but I had a gut sense that, being Jewish, I didn't belong in either, and neither did my kids.

My three siblings and I had gone to public schools, and there had never been discussion of anything else. I knew of a couple private schools in the area, but those were for the rich kids. One of my childhood friends left the public schools for one of these private schools when I started high school. My friends and I thought she was a snob for this decision, which to us implied that our public high school wasn't good enough for her.

John's educational experience included a one-room schoolhouse when his family moved to New Hampshire when he was eleven years old, followed by private high school. On the drive to visit his parents on weekends, we passed the boarding school where he had gone as a day student, a cluster of white clapboard buildings set on a wide, rolling lawn in a small town settled well before the American Revolution. To my midwestern sensibilities, it looked like a movie set from an earlier century. *Foreign territory—no Jews allowed* inadvertently ran through my brain.

When we first met, John's daughter from a previous marriage was eleven years old. I knew she had gone to public school in Boston, and John and I readily agreed that our sons would do the same. We both wanted to expose our children to worlds infinitely more multifaceted than we had experienced in our own respective upbringings. And John understood the community-level fallout from white flight every time he walked through a vacant and abandoned house for his job. Jamaica Plain was full of such houses.

Having two sons who could claim their father's heritage set off multiple alarm bells inside me. It opened a door to the possibilities of private schools, a lifetime job in the family business, summering in New Hampshire, and a sense of entitlement that I thoroughly rejected. Or wished I could. Little did I know how this reaction would haunt me over the years to come, or the impossibility of truly rejecting those benefits that now rolled our way as a family. I had never heard of the concept of white privilege, but I knew enough about class privilege that I wanted nothing to do with it. I had worked since I was twelve years old to pay for piano lessons and overnight camp, things that John took for granted. My father's admonitions to me and my three siblings that he "didn't want to spoil us" was a family joke because we all understood that it was not really an economic option.

I had known the sting of being raised an outsider as a Jew in a predominantly Christian community. My siblings and I carried notes to school half a dozen times every year, notifying our teachers that we would be absent for the Jewish holidays. Some of these absences were for minor holidays that even my Jewish friends barely knew. On those days, we dressed in our synagogue-best clothes, and my mother piled us in the car to attend religious services. My clothes were always hand-me-downs, the services an endless morning of chanting prayers in Hebrew. I hated it. I was perpetually embarrassed, having to explain my school absences to teachers and friends.

I desperately wanted to hide my sons from the unearned advantages made possible by my marriage to John. I didn't want them to become insensitive, elite snobs—not that John's family was any of that. They were humble, hardworking, well-meaning people. But the particulars of their world triggered all of the stereotypes buried deep inside me.

While I came to understand that I couldn't take back my children's access to the wealth and benefits that came with John's family, I wished I somehow could. I wanted my sons to fully appreciate their entitlement within a larger world. I wanted them to feel a sense of responsibility for a broader community where everybody would not have their options. I also understood the values and strengths that come from occasional obstacles in life and from exposure to other cultures and perspectives. I wanted to be sure they experienced those as well.

All of these reservations and desires solidified my resolve to send Ben and Jesse to the Boston Public Schools.

* * *

When I looked into signing Ben up for prekindergarten, the ten-year-old court order that dictated student assignment was still in place. It allowed families to identify several choices from among the schools within their designated assignment zone, after which a lottery allocated seats in each school to ensure racial balance that reflected the demographics of the city. By the time I registered Ben, John and I had researched our options and selected a school we were excited about sending our sons to.

Despite the directive of the school department secretary to send my child to a school where they "needed whites," we didn't choose the John F. Kennedy Elementary School on registration day. But that is where Ben landed six months later. Our first-choice school had filled to capacity before Ben's name came to the top of the list. When I opened the school assignment letter that arrived in the mail, my heart sank. But I quickly rallied to the unanticipated challenge. I knew very little about the Kennedy School, and saw no reason not to try it.

In September 1985, Ben and I headed up Paul Gore Street, his little hand in mine, to his first day of prekindergarten at the Kennedy, the closest school to our Jamaica Plain home. With a new red bookbag strapped to Ben's back and the school assignment letter folded in my pocket, we were ready. For Ben, this was the "big-boy" transition from preschool at the YWCA to a "real" school that took up most of a city block. Excited, he quickened his step as we rounded the corner to the Kennedy School.

The 1960s-vintage school building was uninspiring architecturally but well scrubbed. Latino, African American, and white children filtered in from the surrounding streets, accompanied by mothers and fathers and grandparents, some of the bigger kids walking by themselves. The principal, an older white man with a kind smile, greeted us as we entered, clipboard in hand. It all seemed so . . . normal. Nothing like the horror stories of fights in the schoolyard or indifferent administrators that regularly appeared in my morning newspaper.

I can handle this, I thought. *What's the problem people have with the Boston Public Schools?*

Ben's preschool playmate, Jessica, had also been assigned to the Kennedy. Ben and I found our rhythm in those first couple weeks, stopping at Jessica's house to walk together to school, accompanied by Jessica's mother, Kathryn. Kathryn and her husband, both white, had grown up in the suburbs and found their way to Jamaica Plain when they married. Jessica and Ben chattered alongside Kathryn and me as we compared notes.

On the walk home after school, I tried to gain some insight into Ben's new routine. But as his first days at the Kennedy School turned into weeks, I was mystified by his answers to my question, "What did you do in school today?"

"We drew pictures."

"We sang songs and played."

"We filled out worksheets."

"Some of the boys got into a fight today. . . ."

The last two answers seemed to be the recurring themes. By the time I entered the classroom every day at three o'clock to pick up Ben, the child-sized chairs were upside down, worksheets strewn across the floor, four-year-olds running around throwing jackets and backpacks at each other. The room was a blur of white and brown children in nonstop motion, a din of English and Spanish filling the air. As far as I could see, the reported fights appeared to be benign posturing more than anything.

But I wondered, *How could anyone learn in this environment?* It wasn't encouraging, but I forced myself to remain open-minded. *One way or another, we'll make this work,* I thought.

Ben's teacher moved hopelessly from one child to the next, attempting to tame the storm around her, flustered and totally ignored by her charges. I scanned the mob for Ben, who surfaced red-cheeked and out of breath, as if he had just had a great run at the playground.

Ben didn't seem bothered by the commotion, walking up to one child after another asking about his backpack, which he eventually retrieved from under a table in the corner of the room. He seemed to take the chaos in stride.

This was so different from my own childhood; I had no frame of reference with which to compare it. In the midwestern community where I grew up, the Franklin Village Elementary School was a short walk up the hill from the village center. The kindergarten had a separate entrance, and we each brought a small rug with us to school on which to take naps. I can't remember anything but a calm and peaceful presence. I vaguely recalled a routine to those days that seemed sorely lacking in Ben's Kennedy School classroom.

By the end of September, Ben's kindergarten class had still not settled down. That seemed to be just the way things were in the Boston Public Schools. I held on to my "wait and see" approach, with no real idea of where this would lead us.

My neighbor Kathryn wasn't so accommodating. One Friday morning, she announced that she had transferred Jessica to private school. On Monday, Ben and I were on our own for our morning walk to school.

So this was how it worked when white families bailed on the public school system. *Not me,* I thought smugly.

I placed a few phone calls and learned that schools maintained wait lists for the first few months of the school year. I put Ben on the transfer list for our original choice. Not thrilled with how Ben's kindergarten year was unfolding, I wasn't yet panicked either.

In October, John and I received a letter notifying us that a seat had opened up at the William Monroe Trotter Elementary School, our school of choice. I could hardly wait to tell Ben, sharing the news as I picked him up from school that afternoon.

"Ben, I've got some great news! You're going to be changing schools, to the Trotter!"

"WHY?" he balked. For all its chaos, he was growing used to his Kennedy School classroom.

I had not anticipated this as a possible response to my good news. I needed to convince him it was a move for the better.

"Ben, you're going to really like it there. It's not so crazy and out of control."

"But what do they do with the *bad* kids?" he wanted to know.

His question stopped me short in the middle of the sidewalk.

"Ben, I don't think those wild kids are bad. Your classroom is out of control. It's the teacher's job, just like at your preschool, to tell the kids what to do, to teach them new things and how to behave with each other. Dad and I have visited the Trotter, and I think the teachers there will be better about all that."

Ben listened quietly. He seemed to understand what I was talking about.

This was our first shared lesson in how conditions create "bad" children, and my first of many talks with Ben about good and bad, conditions and circumstances. I was not prepared to believe that a randomly assembled group of twenty-five four-year-olds was inherently bad. But put them in a room with no supervision, and they will run around and get out of control. Multiply this over a ten-year period, and you get a high school full of teenagers with a long history of neglect and behavior that easily translates to "bad." And when such a high school is populated primarily by young people of color, this feeds conveniently into racist stereotypes and a "why bother trying to educate them" attitude. The intervening years become the breeding ground for a self-fulfilling prophecy on the part of those within the school system who are not prepared, willing, or able to create an effective learning environment for these students.

But I'm getting way ahead of myself.

Little did I realize at the time that the simple step I took to apply for a transfer was one of many steps that put my child at an advantage. I did what I had been taught to do by my own upbringing: call the authorities and insist that somebody explain the rules. I filled out the required transfer request and followed up with phone calls every week until a seat became available at the Trotter School.

As I did these things, I had no awareness that this series of tasks might be completely intimidating to many parents. I hadn't yet heard the stories of parents who were less confident or whose skin color or foreign accent triggered outright hostility from school officials. It hadn't yet occurred to me that, for thousands of Boston parents who did not speak English, no written forms and few school department staff could communicate anything at all. I hadn't yet sorted out the relationship between my experience, where in the end I got what I needed for my child, and the lack of responsiveness that had driven black parents to take the school system to court two decades earlier.

As I saw it, by transferring Ben out of a less functional school and into a more successful one, I was safeguarding his success. All parents want success for their children. The fate of the children left behind, through no fault of their own, faded from my view. Yet it sat uneasily in the recesses of my mind, with no ready thoughts of what I might do about it.

CHAPTER TWO

No Crayons, No Paper

"I'M SORRY, BUT YOU CAN'T COME ON THE BUS. I'm not allowed to carry anybody but the students."

The driver matter-of-factly closed the door and stepped on the gas pedal. Before John knew it, the yellow school bus was rolling away down the street. Four-year-old Ben never looked back.

The morning of Ben's first day at his new school, John and I had worried about his transition from walking to taking the bus. Our little four-year-old seemed so vulnerable to be put on a bus with all those bigger kids, especially after our experience at the Kennedy School. Anything could happen. John had walked Ben up the street to the bus stop. Our plan was for John to ride the bus with him, just to be sure everything went smoothly.

As soon as the bus pulled to a stop, Ben centered his little self at the door and hopped on. The driver almost closed the door on John's foot as he attempted to follow.

Ben transferred into the William Monroe Trotter Elementary School in late fall 1985. John and I had been attracted to the Trotter School from the day we reviewed the list of our public school options. It was one of the newer schools in Boston, opened in 1969 in the heart of the black community as a magnet school to encourage voluntary racial integration. The school was named after a black civil rights activist of the late nineteenth and early twentieth centuries. It had a more diverse teaching staff than most Boston schools, which were slowly crawling toward the court-ordered goal of 35 percent teachers of color.

The principal was an African American woman who understood the value of having teachers who looked like the children and shared their life experiences. The school had first opened as a magnet school with a multicultural focus, and it was one of the few schools that taught anything about African American and other cultures.

The Trotter student body was about 85 percent children of color and included African American, Puerto Rican, Jamaican, Chinese, Irish American, Jewish, WASP, and a smattering of other cultures and ethnicities. Many lived with grandparents, single parents, and extended families. These families included middle-class professionals, blue-collar workers, and unemployed welfare recipients. John and I agreed that the school would provide our sons with exposure to a diversity sorely lacking in each of our respective childhoods.

Ben proudly came home from his first days in his new classroom bearing pilgrim hats cut out of construction paper, along with Wampanoag feathers and recipes for the meals that kept the pilgrims alive that first harsh New England winter. He was equally conversant in both sides of the Thanksgiving story. He began to learn his ABCs bilingually, the Spanish version from a parent volunteer who came into the classroom once a week to share her native tongue and customs.

As Ben settled in at the Trotter School, I wanted to encourage his friendships with children of different races. This was the environment I only wished I had had growing up!

Kweku's name kept coming up as Ben came home from school talking about his new friends. I made up my mind to call his parents. Introducing myself to Kweku's mother over the telephone, I suggested the boys get together some Saturday.

Kweku was a lanky, soft-spoken, light-skinned African American boy whose family lived in the Pope's Hill section of Dorchester, a historically white Boston neighborhood just beginning to racially integrate in the mid-1980s. His gentle personality was a far cry from the rowdiness Ben had been surrounded by at the Kennedy School, and better matched Ben's quieter temperament.

My first drive with Ben to Kweku's house took us along Columbia Road, trash-strewn and lined with rundown houses and apartment buildings. I didn't know this part of town, and it didn't look like someplace I'd want to leave my four-year-old for the afternoon. I checked the thought as I glanced at the handwritten directions I had taken over the phone from Kweku's mother, and turned on to Quincy Street.

There go my stereotypes again. What do I know about this neighborhood? Besides, if Kweku lives here, it couldn't be all bad.

I steered our minivan up the hill past a massive stone Roman Catholic Church. Pope's Hill rose gently from the worn main thoroughfares of North Dorchester, its streets lined with century-old Victorian homes whose elegance rose with the height of the hill. My trepidation about leaving Ben to play in the ghetto melted away as I realized that Kweku's house was bigger and more elegant than ours, with a large yard to play in where we had none.

I smiled at myself mockingly.

But something seemed out of place. A hedge in front of the house was blackened and charred along its entire length. Kweku's mother met us with a warm welcome at the front door as we pulled up to the curb. Ben disappeared inside with Kweku.

"What happened to your hedge?" I ventured, dreading the answer I didn't want to hear.

It had been intentionally set on fire when they moved in, Kweku's mother reported with an air of resignation.

Oh. I didn't know what to say other than offering my sympathy and sharing my disgust. It reminded me of how removed I had been from the violence inflicted on black Bostonians when I first moved to Boston. My child's school provided an entry into the lives of those who were still facing the racial hostility, and it made me angry.

What went through the minds of whoever torched this family's front yard?

I couldn't fathom the source of such aggression. And if I had chosen to live in an all-white environment, I might not have believed that such racial violence still occurred.

As I was to learn only much later, U.S. housing policies actively promoted the racial segregation that kept most white Americans buffered from the realities of such racism. Most notable were the policies of the Federal Housing Administration that fueled the post-World War II building of America's suburbs. The FHA, through the Veteran's Administration, offered unprecedented low-interest, low-down-payment mortgages to returning GIs. Mortgage underwriting regulations favored single-family houses and gave more favorable loan ratings to all-white areas. The under-lying assumption was that nonwhite or racially integrated neighborhoods were inherently unstable and made for higher-risk loans.

As a result of this single policy, $120 billion in mortgages underwritten by the federal government allowed a vast swath of white American families to become first-time homeowners. Less than 2 percent of these funds were lent to nonwhite families. Qualifying veterans of color were generally turned down because their communities were rated as too high of a credit risk and because of exclusionary zoning laws that specifically prohibited blacks from moving into most of the new suburban communities.

The trajectory created by this federal policy put families like mine in the suburbs throughout the 1950s and into the 1960s. It allowed us to build wealth in the equity of our homes. That equity allowed my family to weather my father's small-business ups and downs, as he borrowed against our house during tough times. For other white families, this home equity covered college loans or down payments for the next generation, the baby boomers, to buy their first homes.

Being shut out of this source of home-purchase loans left families of color locked behind the starting gate. It wasn't until the Fair Housing Act was signed in 1968 that families of color had a chance to access such home financing. Nearly two decades after that, as my son Ben settled into the Trotter School, the reverberations of such policies were still being felt. And a new round of discriminatory lending was getting underway, which ag-gressively marketed high-interest, unaffordable mortgage loans dispropor-tionately to families of color. This predatory lending triggered the foreclosure crisis of the twenty-first century.

I moved into the city by choice. But decades of housing discrimination had prevented reciprocity for families of color to choose the suburbs. By 1985, cities throughout the United States had become overwhelmingly African American. This racial isolation fueled the ignorance of white Americans about conditions in urban America. If I had followed my par-ents' trajectory, I never would have encountered Kweku's burned-up front hedge. I could easily have believed that racism was a thing of the past and would never have been exposed to any evidence to the contrary.

As Ben got to know his new classmates, I seized the opportunity to meet *my* new schoolmates when a slip of paper came home in Ben's backpack announcing the monthly parent council meeting. On the designated evening, I drove up to the still-unfamiliar school and found a place to park on the dark street. I had only been to the school in the daylight, when school was in session.

Now there was a chill in the air, no outside lighting, and no signage about a meeting. I looked up and down an empty sidewalk, studying a series of dull metal doors. Attracted like a moth to the familiar, I headed toward the kindergarten entrance and tried the door handle. Locked. Methodically working my way around the front of the building, I tried another door. Locked. I took another look around me in the dark.

Was I in the right place?

This was an almost all-black neighborhood that I knew very little about. I began to get nervous. In retrospect, I can see a well-conditioned reaction to nothing more than ignorance and racial discomfort.

The notice couldn't have lied about a school meeting.

Eventually, one door gave way.

Inside, all was quiet. A carpeted lobby gave no clues to the meeting's location. Standing still and unsure, I thought I heard voices—somewhere. Like Alice in Wonderland, I followed the trail of sound through a long corridor, finally stumbling into a brightly lit room full of real people. A meeting was in progress, black and white parents sitting at child-sized tables talking. I had tumbled out the other end of the rabbit hole, back to reality, with relief.

This was my welcome to my son's new school. The experience left a lot to be desired. And this school had a reputation of being one of the best in the city at that time. Once again, I shrugged it off. But on the inside, my indignation was beginning to build.

What kind of a school system is this that can't even point parents to the right door to get inside their child's school for a parent meeting?

I had expected the big-city school system of Boston, new to me and still charged with controversy following court-ordered desegregation, to hold challenges. But the public schools now belonged to me as a Boston resident and parent of school-aged children. If there were problems, I owned them just as I owned my Jamaica Plain home. It seemed simple enough that the responsibility for their functioning rested with the residents of the city. That's why they were called *public* schools. My particular combination of utter naïveté and mission-like zeal were setting me up— for what, I had no idea.

Where did this unquestioning commitment come from? I think back to my father, one evening when I was maybe nine years old, holding up a piece of paper he had just picked up off of the floor. "This paper," he roared at us four kids sitting around the dinner table, "has been sitting on the dining room floor for two days. Every one of you has walked by it, and nobody picked it up! Whose responsibility do you think it is? It doesn't matter who dropped it in the first place. It's *ALL OF YOURS!*"

I knew it was my responsibility to step up when Ben entered his second year of kindergarten, "K2" in Boston Public Schools' parlance. He arrived at school that September to find his classroom at the Trotter School lacking crayons and paper. As a seasoned five-year-old, Ben had matter-of-factly reported the state of affairs over dinner the first week of school.

My fork stopped in midair between plate and mouth.

"You have no WHAT?" I couldn't believe what I was hearing.

How could this be? Who ever heard of a kindergarten classroom with no crayons or paper?

I made up my mind to find out what was going on at the first parent meeting of the school year, scheduled for later that week.

This time, I knew which door was the main entrance and easily found my way to the library where parents held evening meetings. I could count on seeing Natalie, another white Jamaica Plain mother whose son Adam was one of Ben's best buddies from preschool. Like me, Natalie had moved to Boston as a young adult and worked at a nonprofit organization. We regularly compared notes as we learned our way around the Trotter School.

A few other white, middle-class, Jamaica Plain parents were already in the library, waiting for the meeting to start. Their faces were becoming familiar to me, as were the faces of some regularly attending African American parents, who mostly lived in the historically black communities of Roxbury and Dorchester. Names and ages of children, what streets they lived on and the location of those street names, who spoke up and who held back during meetings—all swirled through my head as I tried mightily to learn this new community.

I fought my tendency to hang with the other white parents, all too aware of how easily I slid into sitting next to those who were most like me. I took a seat at a table next to one of the African American mothers and nodded hi just as the meeting was called to order by the parent council co-chair.

When the meeting agenda turned to new business, I raised my hand.

"Has anybody else heard from their kindergarten kids that there are no crayons or paper supplies in their classrooms?"

Several other parents confirmed Ben's report about the nonexistent supplies.

One of the seasoned African American parents of an older student summed up the situation for the rest of us. "That's ridiculous! We need to call Court Street first thing tomorrow morning!"

I learned that Court Street was the downtown location of school department headquarters, the root source of all good and evil in the school system. I struggled to keep up with the acronyms and linguistic shorthand that rolled off the tongues of these parents with older children. Some had children already in high school. They seemed so wise to the ways of the school system.

"Court Street"—I need to remember that one.

Heated debate ensued among the two dozen assembled parents about whether to purchase the needed supplies ourselves or lobby school headquarters.

"We need to get the school system to do its job," a member of the lobby-school-headquarters contingent argued. I think it was Natalie, my white friend who tended toward seeking the moral principle behind the action.

"That sounds good, but what do we expect the kindergarten teachers to do in the meanwhile? That could take weeks, or maybe never!" responded Betty, one of the wise and practical elders, siding with the buy-them-ourselves camp.

I observed the back-and-forth like a tennis volley, the sentiment swaying to this side, then the other, unsure of which side to root for. The opposing camps did not appear to fall along racial lines, and I could see the point from both perspectives.

After nearly half an hour of examining and debating our options, the parent council chair suggested we proceed on both fronts. And I asked myself, *Would this be happening in a wealthier school district—or in a predominantly white school?* It wasn't about the money. According to one parent, who had already broached the subject with the school principal, the budget was in place for supplies, and the order had been submitted on time. The problem appeared to be the central bureaucracy's inability to deliver.

I had no way of knowing whether the breakdown was incompetence or racism. I suspected that the mostly white administrators in charge of the day-to-day workings of the central office were the same people who had resisted years of appeals by the black community for equitable treatment. And I was beginning to think that our experience with kindergarten supplies was exactly the kind of problem that had led black parents to take the school district to court more than a decade earlier.

So this is what inequity looks like, I thought. And what it feels like: insulting, frustrating, and humiliating. And potentially debilitating to our children's education.

If the kindergarteners have no crayons and papers, what's it going to look like in third grade? Eighth grade? High school? What kind of a school system can decide it's okay to start the school year without the most basic of supplies in each classroom?

The lack of crayons that first week of kindergarten turned out to be a preview of things to come. There were the roof leaks that nobody seemed to be responsible for, which led to mildewed carpeting that exacerbated the already high rate of asthma in the school. My wait for the morning school bus with Ben took weeks to settle into a predictable routine. The pickup time on the transportation notice we received in the mail bore no resemblance to the actual time when we saw the bus approaching down Centre Street. I got tired of giving the same excuse as I arrived at work late day after day. Luckily, I worked at a neighborhood nonprofit where nobody docked my pay when I got to work late.

Then there was the day the bus didn't appear at all. Three of us parents talked in circles as we waited at the bus stop, wondering how long we should wait.

"The beginning of last year, there was a day when the bus came a full hour late," offered Barbara.

"I can't afford to wait that long to get to work!" I responded. Thirty minutes was my breaking point.

Maria volunteered to drive the children from our shared bus stop to school. I thanked her and hightailed it to *my* bus stop to get to work, grateful for her offer.

This was crazy. How many hoops does a parent have to jump through to send her children to school?

It was as if the school system didn't *want* people to use it.

I became convinced that some downtown administrators were still secretly staging their protests against school integration through their erratic deployment of the yellow school buses rolling across the city ten years later. There was a whole department that managed transportation. What, I wondered, did they do all day long?

During the first week of school that year, I engaged in elaborate transportation negotiations with school staff and bus drivers. Ben's kindergarten day was only two and a half hours long. Natalie and a couple of other mothers of Ben's preschool friends had tipped me off that my children were more likely to get into our school of choice if we started them in kindergarten rather than waiting until first grade and hoping that seats were still available. Boston only offered half-day kindergarten, which was hardly ideal for working parents. But getting into the right kindergarten was one of the tricks to making the system work. I muddled through the transportation negotiations, annoyed and frustrated that I had to put such effort into getting the most basic of school services at my child's school.

I counted on my network of white, middle-class Jamaica Plain parents to explain the unwritten rules, especially those parents with older children who were a step or two ahead of me in the schools. That's how I learned how to address my kindergarten transportation dilemma.

I didn't learn until years later that many parents of color did not have access to such information. The informal knowledge about how to make the schools work was passed along within mostly white circles. Maybe nobody *planned* it that way; it's just how social networks work. It may well have started intentionally, with elected officials and school department employees who were unwilling to share information and resources with families of color. The lawsuit that led to court-ordered desegregation was only filed after many years during which black families experienced exactly this lack of responsiveness. The informal systems did a good job of continuing to keep people of color on the outside.

But I didn't know or understand all of this as I negotiated for the school bus to drop Ben off at his after-school program. And I hadn't yet figured out how many parents of color did not have the kinds of jobs that allowed them the luxury of taking off in the middle of the workday for a school visit. In my mind, we were all in this together. I was suffering the same indignities as the parents of color. I believed I was truly inside their world—and I was, but not inside their skins. I had a lot more working in my favor than I recognized at the time.

On the first day of kindergarten that year, I took a long lunch break from work to drive to school and introduce myself to Ben's bus driver and Carol, the clipboard-toting school assistant. I found Carol busily lining up the kindergarteners in front of the school, hustling them onto their assigned afternoon buses.

I stepped carefully around the shifting lines of four- and five-year-olds milling around my waist. The last thing I wanted was to disrupt the procedures of the school staff person whose cooperation I now required.

"Is there any way you can have Ben dropped off at his preschool? It's just down the street from his bus stop near our house."

I had arranged for a half-time day-care slot at Ben's preschool to fill the gap in kindergarten hours, and desperately needed a yes.

"I'm not supposed to do it, but sure, I don't see a problem. I think there are a couple of other kids being dropped off there anyway."

Whew. "Thanks so much. I really appreciate it!"

Carol agreed to make a note on the bus driver's route sheet, and I jumped in the car and headed back to work.

This alternative drop-off strategy depended on the reliability and goodwill of these two people to bend the bus rules. It was a workable but fragile arrangement that could be thrown off by something as simple as a substitute bus driver.

That fall, I spent many noontimes at work praying to the school bus gods that Ben would end up at the right place. I shoved from my consciousness the image of my five-year-old son being dumped dutifully at the street corner six blocks from home, at his officially assigned bus stop instead of the preschool where he was supposed to be. I didn't let my imagination dwell on little Ben wandering city streets where anything might happen.

On my morning walks to the bus stop with Ben, I developed a game as my primary line of defense against such possibilities.

"Ben, tell me whose house that is. And that one. And the yellow one at the corner . . ."

Then I would remind him that if he ever needed help, he should ring the bell at one of those houses. In my mind, I reviewed the list to assure myself that at least one of these neighbors was likely to be home at midday.

From my new Jamaica Plain friends, I learned that there were many other parents engaged in the same juggling act. By the beginning of Ben's second year in kindergarten, the issue had risen to the top of the parent council agenda. At the October meeting, the group agreed to send a letter to the central office asking that our informal alternative bus drop-off arrangements be officially recognized. The letter we got back a few weeks later was not encouraging:

> The concept of alternative transportation drop-off for students will be studied and operational recommendations made to the Superintendent for possible implementation in school year 1987-88. Several issues have been raised since September which require further study.
>
> Since your alternative drop-off has begun for 1986-87, the arrangement will be honored for the remaining portion of the school year. However, you should understand that if an alternative drop-off policy is not implemented in 1987-88, your alternative drop-off arrangement will be terminated and siblings will not be eligible.

By bringing our plight to the attention of the central office, Trotter parents were now at risk of losing the informal arrangements we had worked out.

Perhaps we would have been better off staying below the radar screen? I thought with alarm.

Four months later, the school committee voted to approve an alternative transportation drop-off policy. In March 1987 the Trotter Parent Council received a letter from the superintendent of schools informing us that our school was one of six pilot schools selected for the program, which would officially begin the following school year. We rejoiced at our small victory.

Maybe the school system was capable of being responsive to parents after all.

Or maybe not.

I first became aware of the annual scramble for assignment to popular teachers as Ben's K2 school year drew to a close. It started when my phone rang one day in June; my friend Natalie was on the other end of the line.

"Whose class is Ben going to be in next year?" she asked, wanting to be sure her son Adam wasn't without friends in his new classroom in the fall. *How will he make new friends*, I wondered, *if he sticks so closely to his old friends?*

John and I deliberately selected for Ben, and then Jesse, a loosely organized Spanish-language program that moved up through the grades. Our neighborhood was largely Spanish-speaking, and the program would add a relevant complement to the rest of our boys' education at the Trotter. The school had few Spanish-speaking families at that time. The program had been started by Latino teachers with support from a couple of Latino parents.

Although the program's teachers were not the most sought-after in the school, we found them warm and caring. This decision allowed us to circumvent the annual jostling that resulted in the most popular teachers' classrooms being filled with white, middle-class children, leaving the less popular teachers with all students of color.

What started so seemingly innocently—a mother's desire that her child be with friends—provided an unsettling hint of how segregation persists, even within an apparently diverse school. After so many of the white parents finished their advocacy, the children of color landed with the teachers who were perceived by the white parents to be less effective.

The popular teachers tended to be more engaging and creative, and included many teachers of color. One irony in this arrangement was that it allowed the white parents to feel good that they were exposing their children to strong adult role models of color. For me, selecting the Spanish-language track made me feel good that I was at least breaking away from the herd mentality of my white friends. I didn't understand that all of these choices were rooted in our white sense of entitlement and assurance in navigating the system.

As for the racial segregation and inequities that it created, I saw them and didn't like them.

Where did I get such a compulsive sense of fairness? I think back, once again, to childhood. Each of us four children had our assigned days of the week, where we had special responsibilities—setting and clearing the dinner table—and privileges—choosing the TV shows and riding in the front seat of the car. My mother solved the problem of four children divided into seven days by giving the youngest one, my brother David, Sunday. Everybody knew Sunday was the best day of the week.

The parent council at the Trotter School reflected a parallel adult facet of our children's racial divide. Each month that I showed up for a parent council meeting, I was startled anew that attendance was disproportionately white, middle-class parents. I had expected to see a representative sampling of everybody who sent their children to the school and had no idea at the time why that would not be the case.

Natalie and the other Jamaica Plain mothers, Betty and a few other white Dorchester parents, mostly came as "settlers of the frontier," college-educated professionals who had moved into not-yet-gentrified neighborhoods like Jones Hill and Jamaica Plain. During my first few years as a Trotter parent, nobody talked about the gulf between families whose children attended the school and those who showed up at parent meetings. We white parents craved the diversity of the Trotter—but had no vocabulary to discuss the divisions that took place once we got there.

Neither the adult nor student versions of this racial separation seemed right to me. It flew in the face of the reasons John and I had chosen the Trotter School. I could see it unfolding like a slow motion film; I could put together in my mind how it happened. But I didn't have a clue what to do about it.

CHAPTER THREE

Contact Zones

"MOM, COME UPSTAIRS AND LOOK!"

Jesse had been quietly entertaining himself in the bedroom he shared with Ben when he interrupted my Saturday morning housecleaning. I set the mop in the bucket on the kitchen floor and headed up the stairs. Three-and-a-half-year-old Jesse was standing on the upper bunk bed with a heavy rope tied around his waist, the other end tied around the bedpost.

"Mom, what do you think would happen if I jump?"

I always thought there was a particular personality that went with natural redheads. Jesse had inherited his almost-red hair from my mother, along with an independent and creative spirit.

I didn't know whether to laugh or scream. Jesse always had a way of thinking outside the box.

That year, he was finally of age to be eligible for four-year-old prekindergarten, and I promptly enrolled him.

In the fall of 1988, Jesse did not get in to the Trotter with his brother Ben but was instead assigned to the Agassiz Elementary School, the second choice John and I had listed on the application. The day I opened the form letter with his kindergarten assignment, my heart sank. Not only did he not get the sibling preference that was supposed to be built into the assignment policy, but his new school's morning start time was a full hour later than Ben's.

This is crazy.

But what's a mother to do? That fall, I went home in between the two morning bus pickup times and started dinner. I figured I could at least take the edge off the dinner prep at the end of my workday by cutting up a few potatoes at eight thirty in the morning.

The staggered starting times allowed the school system to use their fleet of buses twice to get elementary students to school. It made sense from a budgetary perspective. But I was faced with standing at one bus stop with one child at eight in the morning, then the other one at a different bus stop an hour later, and then somehow getting myself to work on time.

Many parents give up on the public schools at this point. How much inconvenience can working parents take, especially if they believe they have other options? The social sorting continues, rewarding the more advantaged and aggressive who either get out or do what I did next.

For a second time, I put my child on the transfer list, adjusted my routine, and tried to maintain my patience with the school system. Within a couple of months, the transfer notice arrived, and I had two children at the same school.

John was now running a new housing assistance program he had launched two years before Ben was born. He worked long hours, including every Thursday evening and all day Saturday, a sore point between us. All of our talk about equal responsibility in parenting was not panning out as I had been led to believe. I loved my time with Ben and Jesse, but I struggled with the bulk of household chores now falling on me. John sometimes took Ben along to work on Saturday mornings to ease my resentment, setting him up to sell donuts and coffee to customers coming through the door. Ben enjoyed the enterprise, and I only had little brother Jesse to juggle with housecleaning and grocery shopping on those Saturdays.

"Mom, play with me!" Jesse often tried to lure me into his games, splayed on the living room floor absorbed in a pile of wooden blocks or a string of toy trains.

"Not now, Jess ..." I felt guilty that I so often put him off. But how would the laundry ever get done? By Saturday, I could feel the cumulative burden of a long workweek, evenings spent scrambling to get dinner on the table after work before the kids fell apart.

It seemed that every weekday evening as I started cooking dinner, the onslaught of daily injustice reports would begin.

"Mom, the kids in the back of the bus got into a fight this afternoon. And the driver didn't do a thing about it."

Ben pulled his homework out of his backpack onto the kitchen table, always eager to take care of his responsibilities. He matter-of-factly reported the day's news, just a touch of indignation in his voice.

Jesse overheard and chimed in from the next room, where he had parked himself on the sofa in front of the TV as soon as he got through the front door. "You should hear the lunch monitor yelling at the boys at lunch! Almost every day, she makes one of the big kids stay in from recess. Even when they haven't done anything. It's not fair!"

With each week that passed, my sons brought home a new set of problems. My second work shift kicked in as I picked up Ben and Jesse from their after-school program, hustled them into the house, and started fixing dinner.

I made mental notes as I peeled carrots and stirred the pasta. If work the next morning wasn't too busy, I could phone the principal about the bus driver.

Why wasn't there a monitor on their bus?

At the next parent meeting, I'd bring up the problem with the yelling lunch monitor and see if others had heard similar complaints from their children. I found myself constantly reordering my "to do" list based on the facts at hand. Right now, basic safety took precedence over perceived injustice.

I had no awareness at the time of what these seemingly minor injustices represented. Studies have shown that black boys are punished more frequently and more severely than their white counterparts in school districts across the United States. According to one study, they experience almost triple the rate of out-of-school suspensions. If black boys were suspended at the same rates as white boys, there would be half a million fewer out-of-school suspensions of black boys nationally.

Why the disparity?

Whether we believe the stereotypes or not, we all can name them. The angry young black man, always on the verge of violence. We learn to react to this stereotype by clutching our purses a little tighter. Or by jumping too quickly on the smallest infraction of seven- and eight-year-old black boys, while cutting a little slack for the same behavior in white boys, allowing how "boys will be boys."

This simple, often unconscious difference in reaction, by adults of all racial identities, can lay the groundwork for life. The black boys who have been singled out then react angrily to the unfair discipline they encounter. The adults then feel the need to put their foot down with the angry black boys.

Across the country, black boys are referred to special education services at three times the rate of white boys. Most frequently, this is not for a specific learning disability but for "mental retardation" and "emotional disturbance." In 2001, black boys in Connecticut, Mississippi, North Carolina, and South Carolina were four times more likely to be placed in special education than their white counterparts. Other studies have shown Hispanic boys to be close behind black boys in this phenomenon. This early tracking too frequently leads to a trajectory of low expectations and dead-end education. Or to discipline that pushes young people into the criminal justice system.

If we look at the behavior and adult reactions that trigger this path into special education, what sort of an intervention would be more effective? It would be with the *adults*, not the students.

As Monday ran into Tuesday and Wednesday, I had still not found the time to phone the school principal about the fights on the bus. I studied my schedule and decided to squeeze in a trip to school before work on Friday, to talk face-to-face with Carol, the white staff person in charge of the buses.

At 7:45 AM that Friday, Carol stood on the sidewalk in front of the school with her clipboard in hand, barking orders to the children stepping out of the school buses lined up along the curb.

"Hey, Tyrone, no running!"

"Keisha, where's your jacket? Don't you know it's cold today?"

"Christopher, pick up that candy wrapper!"

I waited for a lull between buses unloading and approached her.

"Carol, I'm hearing that Ben and Jesse's bus has gotten pretty rowdy lately. The kids get into fights on the afternoon bus, and the driver doesn't do anything."

Carol rolled her eyes. "Theirs isn't the only one. The problem is that we don't have regular bus monitors anymore. They got cut out of the budget this year."

New information to me. "You mean there are *no* bus monitors?"

"Well, there are a few still on payroll, but not enough for every bus. They get rotated around the system based on who's having the most trouble or who makes the most noise."

I took the name and phone number where the bus monitors were scheduled, thanked Carol, and jumped into my car to get to work. As I drove, I schemed about organizing a group of Trotter parents to weigh in and secure a couple of bus monitors. A temporary solution, but better than nothing.

I was learning the "squeaky wheel gets the grease" approach to improving our schools. I was still unaware that the system was more likely to respond well to me than to a parent of color, despite the fact that I was now using my race and class advantages all the time.

A few Trotter Parent Council members had sent out a survey and got back results that gave the school low marks for communication with parents. Other findings included the need to decrease antagonism between teachers and parents, improve building cleanliness and maintenance, and keep the bathrooms stocked with toilet paper. I noticed Ben and Jesse routinely exiting our home bathroom shaking their wet hands, a technique refined in school bathrooms that were forever lacking paper towels.

One white father, Bob, made it his personal mission to get the school's leaking roof repaired. He doggedly worked his way up the bureaucracy, past our school custodian to the Facilities Department downtown, then on to Capital Planning. I had no idea what he was talking about as he faithfully reported his progress at our school parent council meetings, month after month.

"I talked with Rob Roy for the third time, and he now says that he is not the one who decides which school repairs get funded. Major repairs come out of the capital budget. I think we need to lobby the mayor if we want the roof fixed."

Another parent offered to draft a letter to the mayor.

Who is Rob Roy? I wondered. *And what's a capital budget?* All the problems and proposed solutions seemed so overwhelming.

By the time Jesse joined Ben at the Trotter, I had learned to navigate the school. I knew my way to the library where we held our parent meetings, but still got lost upstairs, where the classrooms were laid out in a confusing maze.

Once a month, faithfully, I made sure John could cover the home detail so I could attend parent council meetings. I got home from work with just enough time for a quick check-in and early dinner if I was lucky. Sometimes dinner wasn't ready, and I left for the meeting on an empty stomach. On those nights, by around eight thirty, I started to lose focus and wondered why my energy was waning.

These meetings were necessary for comparing notes with other parents, organizing, and sharing the tasks of making the school work better for us and our children. They enabled me to get to know the place where my sons spent most of their waking hours. They were also an opportunity to get to know other parents. A distinct side benefit was that Ben and Jesse knew I was around at their school. It kept them honest, knowing I might drop in and talk to their teacher or the principal, unannounced, at any time.

The Trotter had a strong core of parents who showed up regularly for monthly meetings. White parent participation continued to overrepresent our numbers at the school. I was beginning to see how race and class converged, throwing up a host of obstacles to participation for too many families of color. Night jobs, unreliable transportation, and lack of child care were the more obvious obstacles. I was also beginning to see the barrier created by the large number of white, college-educated parents who always seemed to dominate parent meetings. I didn't entirely understand it at the time, but we were intimidating. We left little space for parents who were less sure of themselves to jump in and participate.

My decision to commit to the Boston Public Schools led to a lifetime of learning about race and racism, politics and privilege. Inequity abounded. At seven of the eight schools my children were to attend over the years, young people of color made up 80 to 90 percent of the student body. These schools included a few of the best in the system as well as some known for their mediocrity. Yet, for all their adversity, my sons came through the experience with a sound education and positive sense of themselves. This was not the case for many of their peers.

It wasn't until I listened to parents who were different from me in race, class, and life experience that I saw how a child could go through the same schools as mine, side by side in the same classrooms with the same teachers, and come out with a fundamentally different experience. It wasn't until I took it upon myself to learn more about the long history of intentionally inequitable resources and opportunities that I saw how such different outcomes were about much more than personal choices. This was frightening. It was even more frightening to think I might never have noticed.

At monthly Trotter parent meetings, I was learning how veteran parents worked the system. The letter about alternative transportation had been drafted by Bob, an information technology professional who had done his homework and figured out whom to send it to, how to frame the issue, and how to follow up without ruffling the feathers of sometimes-testy bureaucrats. I suspected this was not typical of other schools that didn't have so many professional parents like us: people with the time, skills, and confidence to sustain such efforts.

While the Trotter core group was disproportionately white, there was a strong contingent of parents of color who were equally active. They tended to be college-educated, much like the white parents who were most involved.

Looking back, our challenges were as much about engaging low-income, less formally educated parents as they were about racial diversity. It doesn't take a college degree to know what's best for your child, and another set of voices would have further enlightened our understanding and actions. The convergence of race and class created the most enduring barriers to parent involvement. There were logistical obstacles for this group, to be sure. But the lack of trust and discomfort with the schools loomed equally large.

As I got to know the regulars at our parent meetings, my own unconscious stereotypes slowly gave way. The parents of color I got to know became real people rather than empty images superimposed with learned stereotypes. Robert, originally from Nigeria, owned and managed investment property in the neighborhoods around the Trotter School. Cynthia, an African American woman with a PhD, worked in public health. Paulina, who was raised in New Jersey by her Puerto Rican parents, was a college-educated community organizer. Debra was a stay-at-home African American mother with a deep understanding of the neighborhood surrounding the school where she had grown up. This was an interesting, thoughtful, committed, and truly diverse group of parents.

As I got to know these parents as individuals, I no longer saw a blank mass of black and brown faces when I entered the room. I saw Robert and Cynthia and Paulina and Debra. I knew that Robert would bring a businessman's critical eye to our projects. Cynthia understood how to maneuver within large institutions. Paulina brought an organizer's skill in turning up the heat when needed, and Debra could make important community connections outside of the school.

Recent research on hidden biases explains my initial reactions. This research, published in 2011, found that more than 85 percent of Americans do not consider themselves to be racially biased. Yet various tests consistently reveal that the vast majority of us do harbor some level of racial prejudices. What is referred to as "implicit bias" affects our actions, even as we are unaware of our own prejudices. This research found that many white people who do not believe they are prejudiced show high levels of implicit bias. They unconsciously view black people as threatening or inferior, which affects how they interact with black people in real situations.

The impact of this can be devastating. Doctors and judges who showed this implicit bias, for example, made decisions that had lifetime consequences for the black people with whom they interacted.

The good news from this research is that most white Americans do not want to be racially prejudiced. The lesson is that we have a lot further to go than most of us realize.

I wasn't able to articulate all of this yet. But I did know that the parent group was making the Trotter a more hospitable and responsive school for all of our children. And I was beginning to differentiate my hidden stereotypes from reality.

Though I was thankful for our successes at the Trotter, I was troubled about all the problems I suspected were not being addressed as successfully at other schools. While some problems we encountered could be addressed at the school level, many were system-wide policy or budget issues. In Boston, the school department budget is determined by the mayor. My sons started their school careers during an era when Mayor Flynn, who had been a vocal opponent of court-ordered desegregation, quietly defunded the public schools year after year.

My thoughts returned to the Kennedy School, which I had left behind when Ben was four years old.

Didn't those children deserve the same resources and attention?

I needed to find an answer, and the citywide parent council seemed to be the place to look. It had been established in 1975 to be the voice for parents in Boston's desegregation effort. When I found the notice for the organization's annual meeting in Ben's backpack one evening, I decided it was time to investigate.

The citywide parents' meeting was held at Madison Park High School, a modern concrete maze with no clear main entrance. *Here we go again*, I thought as I got out of my car, remembering my initial experience at the Trotter. I methodically worked my way along the front of the building in the dark, trying every door until one gave way to my push. Inside, a woman in a security guard uniform sat at a gray metal desk reading a book.

"Is there a parent meeting here tonight?"

She pointed up a set of stairs, mumbled something about a cafeteria, barely looking up from her book.

I was beginning to believe that the school system was telling us parents in every way it knew: *Stay away!*

Fifty to sixty people, mostly people of color, mingled between the long rows of lunch tables in the center of a vast space. A white woman sitting behind a table near the door motioned to a sign-in sheet, then resumed talking with a black woman seated next to her. Not terribly welcoming, I thought. I didn't recognize anybody I knew, and moved to the edge of the small crowd.

I hate this.

I was so far out of my comfort zone, feeling out of place among so many strangers, so few white people, such unfriendly surroundings. I wrestled with a desire to flee.

But I need to be here.

We were all in this together and needed to support each other. I had somehow, misguidedly, thought that any parent who showed up wanting to help improve the schools would be welcomed by the others. I wasn't so sure right now. I fought with my own discomfort about being ignored, feeling out of place in this mostly brown and black crowd of strangers. I stood quietly near the back wall, waiting for something to happen.

About half an hour after the start time stated on the meeting notice, an older black woman stood up and proceeded to describe committees and mandates that I couldn't follow. Some arcane, court-dictated election process for board members seemed to be taking place, as white people were instructed to move into one room, black into another, Hispanic into a third. I dutifully moved into the assigned room, confused as to what was happening.

The white group was the smallest, with fewer than a dozen people. Those who appeared to be longtime board members huddled to one side and talked among themselves. I became very self-conscious, one of very few white people dressed as though they were coming from professional jobs.

Do I belong here? Am I imagining their contempt toward me?

I wanted nothing more in that moment than to disappear. But I believed that we would never effectively solve the problems at the Trotter without a coordinated, citywide approach. At best, we would simply move those problems to somebody else's school. And this was the only place I knew to address school problems systemically.

Despite my discomfort, I returned the next month. Maybe it was my being the third child of four growing up. You learn persistence if you want to be heard.

What I saw as a pattern of disorganization persisted in the monthly meetings I began to attend. A dozen parents filtered one by one into the meeting room, gathering around a large table. Most were African American and older than I was, with children in schools across the city, many with teenagers in high school. One man came in a gray uniform for the night job he went to after the meeting ended. Two women shared notes on the grandchildren they were raising. A cab driver arrived just as the meeting began, on break from his twelve-hour night shift.

Completely out of my element, I watched and listened, trying to understand the range of experiences so different from my own. Race, class, age, neighborhood—so many of the references were unfamiliar to me. I wanted to learn—and needed to understand—these lives and perspectives if I was going to work with this group of parents. I could see a steep learning curve stretched in front of me.

The director, the same older African American woman who had run the elections at my first meeting, walked into the room wearing a tired look on her face. She began her report to the assembled group, which once again I could barely follow. I couldn't hear or see evidence of an agenda; people simply raised concerns as the thoughts came to them.

"Did anybody hear about the fight at Dorchester High School last week?"

High school seemed so far away to me, I had a hard time relating. The details reminded me of the unsupervised four-year-olds at the Kennedy School—what they might become ten years later. Another parent interrupted my thoughts.

"That new reading program they're introducing—it doesn't work for black children. It's not the right way to be teaching our kids."

I knew nothing about reading programs.

"Did you know, at my son's school the principal kicks the parent council out of the building whether we're through with our meeting or not?"

What felt to me like random conversations continued until it was time to go home. Nobody appeared particularly troubled that none of the problems were actually addressed. It didn't occur to me at the time that the simple sharing of concerns may have been just as important as what I viewed as problem solving. I had no idea how great my gap in understanding was.

From my limited experience, there seemed to be something wrong. But was the problem the organization? Or me? I was working in a community organization whose staff put a lot of care into how meetings were run, making sure agendas were clear, that everybody had a chance to speak, that decisions were arrived at. This felt like a poster child for an ineffective meeting.

Was I being too judgmental of this organization I knew so little about, these people whose life experiences were so different from my own?

I asked around among my white friends at the Trotter. I wasn't yet sure of myself about anything to do with race, and I avoided asking the Trotter parents of color. I worried that sharing my reservations about the citywide group might expose me as a racist. I didn't understand the dynamics of the organization or of racism. Rather than expose my ignorance, I retreated to more familiar ground. I felt safer asking other white parents. I assumed, whether rightly or wrongly, that they were more likely to understand my reactions. This meant that the interpretations I got were most likely to be similar to my own, reinforcing any differences in perspective along racial lines.

From my poking around, I gleaned a bit of the backstory. Funded under a federal court mandate, the organization's role was to ensure black and Latino parent involvement in school system changes. I knew this much from the materials handed out at the annual meeting I had attended. In its early days, deep funding had supported an army of staff, cab vouchers, and child care to help low-income parents attend evening meetings at their children's schools across the city. This was a critical component of opening the public schools to families of color, eliminating the barriers that had been placed in their way for so many decades by the Boston School Committee.

By the time I got involved with the group, it had a complicated reputation, fiercely protected by many people who understood its roots, while appearing to have limited effectiveness at mobilizing parents to improve the schools. It was unconditionally supported by many, including most groups and individuals in the African American community. While I did not fully understand this unwavering support, I knew that challenging the organization's effectiveness was akin to an act of treason.

If the organization was founded to support the leadership of parents of color, what did that mean for me? I wanted to help but was unsure how, other than showing up for these monthly meetings.

By 1990, my world revolved around showing up at monthly Trotter parent meetings and monthly citywide parent meetings. I spent a lot of time listening, trying to understand these worlds that were so different from the one I had been raised in. I had a gut sense that the parents of color should be in the leadership roles. They were the ones who had experienced so much hostility over the years, the decades, the generations. I assumed they knew best what was wrong and what was needed to make things right. It was their turn to take the lead.

That spring, as the weather warmed up and the tulips and daffodils began to poke out from the thawing earth, the Trotter School held its annual field day. Students, teachers, and family members milled around the paved schoolyard, glad at last to throw off heavy winter coats and mingle. I reveled in the excuse to take a few hours off from work, happy to be serving the food delivered in big foil pans potluck-style by dozens of parents. A small cluster of girls hovered over the far end of the food table, comparing notes on the lunchtime offerings.

"My grandmother makes chicken just like that!"

"That's just like my grandmother's chicken!"

"That's just like *my* grandmother's chicken!"

Despite their grandmothers' different heritages—Puerto Rican, African American, Chinese American—their chicken recipes were common currency. These were the moments that affirmed why I sent my children to the Boston Public Schools. Like these girls, I was comparing notes and delighting when I discovered commonalities.

I was also learning that experiencing diversity wasn't that simple. Too many of us white parents wanted diversity without adversity. And adversity too often goes hand in hand with being poor and living in a low-income community of color.

As spring turned to summer that year, Humboldt Avenue, the street in front of the Trotter School, emerged as ground zero in the erupting gang warfare of Boston. One of the more prominent gangs bore the street's name. A shooting in the park adjacent to the schoolyard one afternoon took tensions to a new level.

"Mom, did you hear what happened after school today?"

I hadn't heard, not until I picked up Ben and Jesse at their after-school program. They had been indoors, but other children were playing outside when the shooting occurred next door. It was out of view but within earshot. Nobody had been killed, or even hurt, but that was hardly reassuring.

My heart jumped into my stomach when I heard the news. *What is happening to our city? This is madness!*

Word spread quickly among the parents through phone calls. Within a week, there was one less child on Ben and Jesse's school bus. I learned from a friend that one of my white neighbors had promptly transferred his son out of the school.

I was terrified but shoved the feeling deep in the back of my brain. All the children couldn't up and leave. Even if most could, what would happen to those left behind? Someone was always left behind in these scenarios, usually the children who had no choice in the matter.

I knew a little about what it felt like to be left behind. During my own elementary school years, my mother forgot to pick me up after school—I don't know how many times, but the memory of it holds clear. It would have been on a day when I was instructed not to take the bus home because I had a doctor's appointment. I waited for my mother at the curb outside the school office. And waited. I remember the principal leaving the building, locking the door behind, and my heart sinking. Would I have to sit on the curb all night? How could my own mother forget me?

It was the loneliest feeling ever. Eventually she arrived, apologizing for her lateness. She worked with my father in his building contractor business and must have gotten caught up with something.

Being left behind was no fun.

My response to the violence and families fleeing the Trotter was to become more active in the school parent council. I began to wake up at night with a start at every little street noise. I lay awake for hours, listening to the creak of the old stairs, half-dreaming a cold pair of hands reaching for my body. In the morning, I hovered at the bus stop like a mother hen over her brood as my sons and the other neighborhood kids waited for the school bus, directly across the street from a known drug house. I couldn't stop bullets from flying, but my sensors went on high alert that year.

In the midst of this chaos, a small miracle happened. Ben was now in third grade, and the newspaper shouted the news that Nelson Mandela was coming to town. Mandela had just been released from twenty-seven years in South African prisons. The African National Congress was engaged in the final and most violent period of resistance to majority democracy, and Mandela was being positioned to become president of a new South Africa.

The Trotter chorus was invited to perform at a dinner gala in Mandela's honor at a downtown hotel. Parents of chorus members filled out forms with our children's Social Security numbers for a mandatory security check. We followed strict instructions about where to meet the bus that took the children downtown, milling around on the sidewalk fixing their stray hairs and retucking white dress shirts as only a parent can do properly. We watched in awe as the bus pulled away with the Trotter chorus members inside.

Late that evening, as parents huddled in the dark waiting for the bus to return, I thought, *This is why I'm proud to send my kids to the Trotter School.* This was not an opportunity that came to just any school, and I was thrilled that my child could be a witness to such history in the making.

When the bus arrived, the young chorus members stepped out, one by one, many of them holding their right hands up in the air. Ben stretched his out in front of me. "Nelson Mandela shook my hand! I'm never going to wash it again!"

The school year ended on that high note.

In August John and I piled the boys into our van for our annual vacation at John's family cottage in New Hampshire. We had brought along Ernesto, one of Ben's closest friends. I knew Ernesto rarely had other opportunities to get out of the city. Ben was glad to have a playmate along. As we left the hot city behind, the car loaded with boys and duffle bags and groceries, the anticipation mounted as we wound through the wooded back roads of New Hampshire. We pulled up to the cottage, and the three boys tumbled out of the car and ran down the driveway to the water's edge.

Ernesto immediately spotted the canoe lying in the grass.

"Can we go canoeing?" His eyes were wide.

I sorted through the orange life jackets hanging on pegs on the porch and found the right sizes for Ernesto and Ben. They dragged the canoe to the water's edge, flung off their sneakers, and climbed into the boat, Ernesto in the rear seat. He handled the paddle like a pro.

When they got back to shore, it was my turn to be wide-eyed.

"Ernesto, where did you learn to canoe like that?"

"In the pool at the Boys and Girls Club!"

Ernesto lived with his mother, younger brother, and older sister on the top floor of a three-unit apartment building in the Four Corners section of Dorchester, one of Boston's poorest and toughest neighborhoods. That fall, Ben played at Ernesto's house as much as Ernesto played at ours, and I spent drop-off and pick-up time chatting with his mother, Judy, a stay-at-home African American mother. Judy baked and sold cakes to supplement her welfare checks.

Ernesto was chubby and inquisitive, quick to share with anybody who would listen his fantasies about becoming a musician or a tai chi master. He took apart and rebuilt everything electronic he could get his hands on. When our old television died, he convinced me to give it to him instead of putting it in the trash. He got it going again and made a place for it in his bedroom.

As I walked up the dingy stairs to Ernesto's apartment, I felt over-dressed and out of place. Coming straight from work to pick up Ben, I sensed that my tailored wool pants and blazer didn't seem to fit into these surroundings. I was more self-conscious about our economic than our racial differences. Judy met me at the door in her jeans and sweatshirt. When I explained that Ben wouldn't be around to play during school vacation because we were going cross-country skiing in New Hampshire or taking the train to Colorado to visit my sister, I was keenly aware that Judy rarely left the city. I imagined that each day bled into the next for her, without the markers of going off to work or away for vacations. I knew these were *my* ways of marking time, but I couldn't fathom hers.

Judy and I worried together about the age-old battles of sibling rivalry. We shared recipes and tips about bargain children's clothing stores. We talked about how things were going at school—all the things mothers talk about. Despite my self-consciousness, I was learning that we had plenty in common. But my heightened awareness of our differences kept me from going deeper. Perhaps if I was less self-conscious, we might have gotten to a more intimate friendship. I can't know that now. Instead, I became more aware of the complexities of building friendships across the divides of race and class, even as my comfort level edged up a notch or two.

Ernesto's neighborhood made the news regularly for drug dealing and street violence. I continued to take Ben to play there, sometimes wondering whether I would regret it if something were to happen to him. I put these concerns out of my mind.

If Ernesto and his family can deal with it, why can't we?

One day, a man was shot dead by police as he ran down the street behind Ernesto's house. When I picked up Ben at Ernesto's that evening, he barely got out the door before blurting out, "Mom, the police killed someone right behind Ernesto's this afternoon!" This was beyond the norm we had grown to expect. But, to the kids, it was just the way things were in Four Corners. I, too, grew to accept this as just the way things were in our world.

I say "our" world, but where was the white world's reaction to this violence? I began to take notice of the much rarer acts of violence in white suburbs, how counselors swarmed in to help the children cope, how these incidents weren't blamed on a culture of violence or the perpetrator's race, as they were when they occurred in the black community. How had we come to this state in which most of us, of all races, somehow found this level of inner-city violence acceptable? Where were the counselors prepared to help these children sort out the violence around them?

At a parent meeting, Trotter parents discussed the need for this type of support. I volunteered to attend a faculty meeting at the Trotter to ask the question.

"We need to do something, to talk about what's going on with the kids. We can't just let it go and expect that it won't affect them."

I was not prepared for the reaction of the teachers.

"We don't have the skills to raise these problems in our classrooms."

"It would be more dangerous to talk with the kids than to let it go. We would be opening up a topic we are not adequately prepared to do anything about."

Stonewalled.

Maybe their assessment of their limitations was accurate. But leaving a vacuum in the wake of the street violence hardly seemed acceptable.

I thought back to Kweku's front-yard hedge, set on fire to let his family know they weren't welcome in that historically white neighborhood. Kweku's family had moved back to the Midwest, where his father was from, a year or two after this incident. Was the move due to the racism they encountered in Boston? I don't know. By the time his family left town, Kweku and Ben had moved on to different classrooms and other friendships.

I thought further back, to the decades of lynchings that white families came out to watch, toting their picnic baskets, throughout the South.

Did we really believe that black-on-black crime grew out of a vacuum?

How were we ever going to create unity across races if we couldn't find the resources and political will to intervene in this endless cycle?

* * *

By second grade, Jesse had transitioned from my hand-knit sweaters to Celtics sweatshirts, his curly red hair made less conspicuous by his insistence that it be cut short—very short. He had become aware of the need to fit in. But fit in with whom? The majority of his classmates were African American. Many of the boys wore their hair in "high tops," shaved on the sides and rising straight up an inch or two on top. We tried to copy the style the best we could with my home hair-cutting equipment, two parallel straight lines cut neatly into each side of Jesse's closely shaved head just above the ears. Yet we both knew that Jesse didn't really fit in, at least not with the dominant culture. This was about more than his hair.

In spite of my earlier zeal about wanting my children to experience a more diverse upbringing than my own, I didn't want them to feel like complete outsiders. To me, it seemed that fitting in would have been so much easier in a school where there was such diversity. At Jesse's school, there was a dominant group of low-income African American families to which we would never belong. At the same time, there was so much variation within that group and beyond.

Jesse's friendships evolved based on shared interests and temperaments. The cultural markers that I so self-consciously tracked were to him merely backdrop. Would I ever get past my heightened awareness of racial and cultural differences? Or should I?

I continued to teach my boys to get phone numbers of new friends. I then piled my kids into our minivan and followed the handwritten directions taken over the phone from unknown parents in unknown parts of the city, pushing back my fear of taking Ben or Jesse to neighborhoods I thought of as rougher than ours.

Jesse's friend Christopher lived in one of the hundreds of apartments in the brick buildings that went on for blocks surrounding Franklin Park. Only one mile from our house, the area was mostly poor, mostly black, and high-crime. When I dropped Jesse off to play, I often wondered what it was like to live there. I scanned the block, which quietly defied my image of what "crime-ridden" should look like.

Christopher and his big brother, Roberto, lived under strict instructions from their mother to stay inside their apartment. She was Haitian, petite, and away at work day and night, working two nursing home jobs to make ends meet. Her options for where she could afford to live placed her in a neighborhood that I considered violent. Our phone conversations rarely went past logistical arrangements for getting our sons together, her voice with a tired edge.

What I pieced together, mostly from her sons, was how their life wasn't so much different from ours. Their mother went to work; they stayed home, did their homework, watched TV. But I had to admit that it *was* different. Christopher and Roberto's unsafe neighborhood and their mom's long work hours limited their exposure to opportunities—opportunities I took for granted, like taking my children to New Hampshire or the beach or a museum or outdoors to the park to play on a sunny day.

My sons' friendships helped me to understand that the vast majority of people in neighborhoods like Christopher and Roberto's were decent, hardworking people simply trying to get by, not what was portrayed in the daily newscasts, where crime and drugs and violence figured so prominently.

The children of such parents did not resort to drugs or violence, although the small handful who did always seemed to be the ones who stood out. Jesse had two or three disruptive students in his class of twenty-eight. At times, they held everybody else hostage. The boy who ran drugs for his older cousin could stop the class with his anger, and he knew it. His accusation of "Teacher, he took my pencil!" would become a shouting match with the teacher, who then tried her best to calm him down. When his acting out escalated to throwing a chair at another student, the teacher had to call in backup from the classroom across the hall. Twenty or thirty minutes of teaching lost, while the rest of the students took in the drama. Jesse, along with most of his classmates, wished the disruptions would just go away.

One day in third grade, Jesse came home with a look of concern on his face; he was not his usual carefree self. A girl in his class had confided in him during library period that afternoon. As soon as we sat down for dinner, he blurted out the story he had barely held in for the last hour.

"She told me that her cousin isn't getting her medication and her mother is doing heroin. She started crying, and I didn't know what to do!" Jesse was close to tears as he conveyed the conversation across our kitchen table.

"It's so terrible. I barely know her—we're not even friends. I felt so bad. I didn't know what to say."

John and I tried to reassure him. "There really isn't a lot you can do, although just being there and listening may have been helpful. We'll call the school in the morning; they should know this is going on and should be able to do something to help her." The next day I reached the principal on the phone. The school counselor knew about the problem and was doing what he could to help.

I wondered how any child in her situation could come to school prepared to learn. And I was thankful that the Trotter was one of the few elementary schools in Boston with a full-time guidance counselor.

Meanwhile, the Trotter Parent Council piled up some significant victories in the midst of the growing chaos. The schoolyard project started when a white parent heard about funding available for playground equipment, announcing the grant at a parent council meeting. Wouldn't it be nice to get rid of the concrete where the children were endlessly scraping knees and elbows?

A couple of parents with grant writing experience signed up to write the proposal for funding. The grant award a few months later spurred the parent council into action. The council needed to form a playground committee. A parent volunteered to head up the effort and drafted an announcement for recruits that went out on one of those little slips of paper forever hiding in the corners of our children's backpacks.

For the first time in my experience, fathers began to show up. Committee meetings were held before school, agendas filled with the logistics of concrete removal, delivery of topsoil and wood chips, and installation of play equipment. It was all business. This project drew a new crowd.

As a playground committee member reported progress at a parent council meeting, I made the mistake of commenting, "Why are the men showing up all of a sudden to help? Where have they been?"

"What do you mean? It's great to see the fathers get involved!" An African American mother sitting at the table next to mine delivered a reminder that diversity isn't only about race and class and ethnicity.

And this was the year that Bob got the leaking school roof onto the city's annual capital budget priority list. Repairs were finally underway. Bob had launched this campaign when his son, who was now in middle school, had been in second grade.

I guess you have to learn patience in this work of holding schools accountable, I thought. And as a white person trying to understand the many-layered dynamics of racial inequities, I needed patience about the fact that I would always be learning.

CHAPTER FOUR

Two Steps Foward, One Step Back, Repeat

I WALKED INTO THE TROTTER SCHOOL LIBRARY and that familiar sinking feeling crept over me, moving from my stomach up to my brain. The room was full of white, middle-class parents, right on time, ready for the parent council meeting to begin. The dolls lined up on the top of the bookshelf along one wall mocked the moment: their miniature figures dressed in the clothes of different cultures, their colorful head garb belying the not-so-multicultural scene below. We, the real people, squished our (mostly white) butts into chairs designed for children half our size.

This was the year Ben started fifth grade: 1991. Klare and I had been elected cochairs of the school parent council. Our parent organization still followed the rules laid down by the federal court order more than fifteen years ago, electing one white cochair and one black cochair. As we waited to start the parent meeting, I looked nervously at Klare. She always seemed so calm.

We could start the meeting on time or wait for a few more parents of color to show up. I was learning the relative meaning of "on time."

We waited.

Klare and I first got to know each other through attending parent meetings and realizing that our sons Eric and Jesse were in the same grade and played together at the Trotter after-school program. She had grown up in the community adjacent to the Trotter, with a prominent mother who was one of the first African American newscasters in the local media. I'm sure my comfort level with her had at least something to do with her middle-class upbringing. And her comfort level with the school had something to do with the private schooling she had received, where learning how to interact with authority was embedded in her education. Klare worked for a local philanthropic foundation and was always gracious under pressure. I don't think I ever heard her raise her voice, or if she did, it remained gentle yet firm.

One day early in the school year, Klare had an observation to share with me.

"You know, many of the black parents feel like the white parents treat them like they're all on drugs or something."

Klare had a way of presenting concerns that got right to the point. Her willingness to share information like this helped me realize how big the gap really was between white and black parents. Up until then, I had sought out the other white, middle-class parents at the Trotter to help me understand school challenges. My relationship with Klare began to shift my thinking about who had all the answers—and what the right questions were. Without her willingness to enlighten me, I might have moved through my sons' years at the Trotter with a much narrower, and sometimes misguided, perspective.

I've since learned the inevitable paradox in this type of relationship. We white people need people of color to play the role Klare played with me, to let us in on other ways of viewing a situation or the world. Yet this relationship puts the responsibility on people of color to bare their pain to us in order for us to learn and grow. It was only years later that I became more mindful of not expecting people of color to do our work for us. Instead, I learned that we can actively seek to understand a situation by paying more attention to how different people act and react around us. We can raise the questions and listen to other people's answers. We can make space for others to formulate the questions. I'm not sure I had done much of this before getting to know Klare.

The idea that white parents at the Trotter tended to keep their distance from parents of color didn't completely surprise me. It was hardly a well-kept secret, even as I was at a loss how to respond. "So what do you think we can do about it?"

Klare and I spent hours talking about how we might conduct business to enlighten the parents—in this case, to get the white parents to back off from dominating both the process and the content of our meetings, and to encourage parents of color to feel that they belonged and had ownership in the parent organization. A complicated balancing act ensued. Neither of us believed that white parents *shouldn't* be active. Klare was helping me understand how the perceived overzealousness of the white parents created barriers to the participation of others.

I didn't know at the time that this pattern was a common one that played out in schools across the country.

It was only years later, when I made it my business to learn about the civil rights movement, that I better understood the long history of racial barriers to educational participation in the United States. Families of color were denied access to quality schools by law for hundreds of years. In many states and cities, it was only through federal lawsuits like the one filed in Boston that they were allowed in to schools with better resources. The NAACP's best-known lawsuit, *Brown v. Board of Education*, filed in 1954, actually consisted of six separate cases targeting four different states plus the District of Columbia. These lawsuits continued well into the 1970s across the country. Even after the courts ruled that segregation and inequitable education were unconstitutional, families of color faced widespread white resistance and violence.

Did we really expect such a long history of hostility to not affect people's willingness to show up for our parent meetings? I'd be wary, too, if only ten years earlier my people had been met with bricks and curses trying to send their children to school and if, for generations before that, they had been denied access to quality schools by the laws of the land.

Klare and I finally put the topic on the agenda at a parent council meeting. I was nervous and unsure what to expect when I saw the agenda item starkly stated on the meeting flier: "How to increase involvement of parents of color." A last minute *Oh no, what have we done now?* flashed through my mind.

When we took up that item, an uncomfortable silence settled over the room.

"What if we say right on our meeting notices that we need more parents of color?" one black parent timidly suggested.

That was about as far as the first conversation went. I silently questioned whether such a simple act would change such a well-entrenched pattern, but I was not about to dismiss any suggestions offered.

Klare and I brought up the issue again at the next meeting. Another parent pointed out how hard it was to get to our meetings on time. When she arrived late, she couldn't follow what was going on.

After that, we wrote each meeting's agenda on the blackboard in the front of the room. Another simple step, this gave latecomers a better idea of where we were on the agenda when they entered the room.

The continued awkwardness of these conversations made it clear that part of the problem was that the majority of people of different races didn't *know* each other.

One evening, Klare and I opened the meeting with a new announcement. "Welcome to the Trotter School Parent Council. We'd like to start by asking you to turn to someone you don't know, introduce yourself, and tell them a little about your children who attend the Trotter."

Few parents can resist talking about their children. The room instantaneously broke into dozens of animated conversations. In the din that rose up in the school library, Klare and I were barely able to bring the meeting back to order. Bingo. We had hit on something here. That simple act of conversation broke up the tension of strangers sitting in undersized chairs at undersized tables waiting for our meeting to begin.

Little changes like this accumulated and produced the desired effect—reinforced by Klare's long-standing neighborhood relationships that built trust with many of the parents of color. Over the ensuing months, the number of parents of color regularly joining our meetings grew.

And they began to point out new agenda items for the parent council to take on. "Why is it that the school chorus has so many white kids? And the school newspaper and student council?" A more representative group began to shift agenda topics to include issues of equity.

The group decided to launch its own research on how the privileges of the school were distributed to students. In fact, all of these selective activities were comprised of predominantly white children, year after year. We wanted to know why.

A few parents, African American and white, agreed to survey the teachers about how they selected children for the identified activities. All the teachers interviewed insisted that they used "objective" criteria or "fair" practices based on good behavior, grades, and an active interest. A few got extremely defensive that we were questioning them at all.

One day during our research, Klare found a Post-it note on the teachers' room wall. "The parents are taking over the school," it read. It appeared that teachers of all races didn't want to talk about race any more than the parents had.

Despite the resistance, a pattern emerged. Many of the white parents were quite comfortable aggressively advocating for their children, who only had to overhear their parents' conversations over the years to internalize a set of expectations concerning what they deserved. It probably started with that first trip to the school office, small child in tow: "I need to talk to the principal." While other parents sat glumly waiting in hard metal chairs, these parents knew how to get heard. They phoned in June to put in their order for the best teacher for the following school year, while other parents hoped for the best. They stopped by in September to meet each new teacher, while many parents of color didn't think this was necessary—or didn't believe they would be welcome.

On top of these differences in behavior and expectations, we all carry our own image of what potential in a child looks like, acts like, and dresses like. The quiet girls dressed in hand-me-downs who stayed up too late at night watching their baby brothers while their mothers were at work, and the rowdy boys imitating their big-brother gangbangers, did not fit the criteria for selective school activities. The teachers, black and white, had all listed criteria for participation—motivation, eagerness, cooperation—that were the opposite of what most adults would see in children like these.

Are these circumstances the fault of the children? I wondered. I thought school was supposed to be the great equalizer. If what was going on at the Trotter was typical of other schools, it was a guarantee that many children raised in tough situations would not get the very things they most needed to motivate their learning and improve their lives.

The extracurricular activities in question were a strong selling point of the school. In most cases, they only happened because of the volunteer time and commitment of the teachers involved. The principal, Ms. Leonard, took no action when we suggested she challenge their practices. Klare and I decided she was probably unwilling to risk losing their goodwill. We both respected Ms. Leonard, an African American mother of elementary school children. She always made herself available when we asked, and kept out of our way when we didn't. She also showed a strong sense of fairness in how she handled the children. We agreed to let go of these particular items.

We then turned our attention to classroom assignments.

When the parent council started to investigate, we discovered that some parents routinely lobbied the school principal in June for their preferred teacher for the following school year. Many of the white parents wanted their children to be in classrooms with their friends, who were more often than not the other white kids. This resulted in a large group of white students moving from year to year through the school in a herd, so to speak.

Klare and I invited Ms. Leonard to a parent council meeting to discuss how students were assigned to classrooms. We had not yet had any explicit conversations with her about the racial inequities we had observed, but we knew where she stood by the way she managed the school. She took the time to find out what was really going on with the African American boys who always seemed to be blamed for transgressions, real or imagined. She listened equally well to the aggressive white parents but didn't readily bend to their demands.

The discussion that unfolded exposed the practice of advocating for favored teachers, widespread among white parents. Nearly every parent of color in the room shook their head or otherwise expressed surprise when Ms. Leonard explained how parents reached out to her every June; they had no idea that lobbying for specific teachers was an option.

I was stunned at the racial divide this exposed.

Reflecting on this meeting years later, I wonder if it also exposed differing values. I have found that white parents are more likely to approach their children's education from an individualistic, competitive perspective. If we aren't first in line, we won't get the best. We will lose in the game of life. We don't often look at what else we lose by focusing so narrowly. Is our quality of life really better if only a few get ahead? What price do we pay as a democracy when our institutions only support and reward the most aggressive among us?

Communities of color often revolve around a more collective definition of success. Many African Americans wouldn't have survived in this country without banding together to support each other. Most immigrants rely on extensive community networks of support to succeed as well. Our country's fixation on rugged individualism is not universal. In fact, one of the countries that is currently viewed as among the most successful at delivering a universally high-quality education, Finland, demonstrates a very different set of values. The country's school system is built on cooperation. There are no lists of "best" schools or poorly performing teachers. When the country embarked on school reform decades ago, the goal was equity, not excellence.

Since the 1980s, Finland's focus has been on ensuring that all children have equal opportunity to learn, no matter what their economic or social circumstances. There is no required standardized testing of all students. There are no private schools in Finland. "There is no word for accountability in Finnish," according to Pasi Sahlberg, director of the Finnish Ministry of Education's Center for International Mobility. "Accountability is something that is left when responsibility has been subtracted." In Finland, teaching is a highly respected profession. If there are problems with teacher performance, it's up to the principal to identify them and address them. Based on an international survey conducted every three years, Finland has for years rated among the top performing countries in math, reading, and science.

This approach flies in the face of our American obsession with competition. Yet the disparate educational outcomes are hard to dispute. I knew nothing of this when Trotter parents faced off with Ms. Leonard about how students were assigned to classrooms each year.

The practice of individual lobbying for a handful of teachers was now on the table at the Trotter School. What would happen if everybody engaged in this lobbying? We knew that we all couldn't win that game. Ms. Leonard suggested an alternative, and we arrived at a new way of assigning students to classrooms.

The new procedure encouraged parents to send a note to the principal at the end of the school year describing the type of teacher and learning environment they believed would be best for their children. The school staff then reserved the right to make assignments to ensure the best possible matches for all students. This put pressure on the active parents and the parent council to be sure all teachers were of a quality we would want for our own children. Parents could no longer guarantee what teachers their children would get.

The discussion that led to this compromise was strained yet civil.

"I don't know about this," one white parent spoke up. "I want to know who my children are going to have for their teachers." She had two children at the school and a younger one on the way. "If I can't continue to pick their teachers myself, I'm leaving this school."

She didn't follow through on the threat, but I appreciated her honesty. There were undoubtedly other parents who had every intention of continuing to lobby the principal but weren't willing to say so out loud.

This was one of my first lessons in the "entitlement gap"—the vast difference in experience and understanding about what one is entitled to in one's interactions with the system.

John and I avoided the annual scramble for classroom assignments by choosing the Spanish-language track for Ben and Jesse. But when Ben got to fifth grade, we faced a dilemma. The Spanish program did not extend into fifth grade. Ben was assigned to a teacher who, the first week of school, asked his students if the homework was too difficult. In a chorus they responded "YES!!" as any self-respecting group of ten-year-olds would. He eased up on their assignments in response.

I was not trained as a teacher, but as a parent I knew that the adult role is to establish expectations and set limits. Ben and Jesse had had teachers up until that point who understood this. Ben's final year at the Trotter was beginning to look like a throwaway.

Arranging an hour off from work, I drove over to the school to talk to the teacher in question. I introduced myself and tried to sound nonaccusatory, probably not very successfully.

"I haven't seen much homework and was hoping I could hear about your homework policy."

He had a vague and unsatisfying response, and I could see that this was not going to be an academically challenging year for Ben. We had had a good run at the Trotter. One seriously deficient year out of seven wasn't bad odds for the Boston Public Schools. I thanked him and decided to let it go.

Until Ben's fourth grade teacher, a young Latina woman relatively new to teaching, called me at home one evening the following week.

"You have *got* to get Ben out of that class," she insisted. While I was prepared to accept that Ben's last year of elementary school was going to be academically mediocre, she was not. "Can't you see how miserable Ben is?" she persisted.

He hadn't said a word to me.

I thanked her, hung up the phone, and went to Ben's bedroom, where he was whipping through his homework of simple worksheets.

"Ben, I just got a call from Ms. Rodriguez. She said you aren't too happy with your teacher this year."

Ben hesitated as a hint of tears emerged in the corner of his eyes. He slowly nodded his head, still looking down at his worksheets.

A long talk confirmed that he was indeed unhappy. At ten years old, Ben had apparently absorbed my own habit of toughing out the challenges, sorting out the things you stand a chance of changing from those you don't. Children can be unsettling mirrors of our own behavior that way.

I scheduled an appointment with Ms. Leonard. It was the first and only time I ever attempted intervention in the classroom assignments for my own children. I could barely sit still in my seat as I faced her desk in the principal's office.

I shouldn't be doing this.

I scanned her face for clues as she patiently heard me out. I explained how I had met with the teacher in question and did not feel that he was being responsive to the academic needs of the students. I wasn't sure if I imagined a struggle pass briefly through her eyes. Or was that a reflection? When I finished talking, she paused for a brief eternity. Then she offered to switch Ben into a different classroom, one of the most popular teachers in the school.

As a result, Ben's last year of elementary school was the best ever.

I never would have intervened if Ben's fourth grade teacher hadn't prodded me with such urgency. I followed the school's procedures, first attempting to address the problem directly with the teacher. When that didn't work, I went to the principal, uneasy about asking for special consideration. In the end, my embarrassment didn't stop me. My values and principles had been tested throughout my years of involvement in the Trotter School. This was the first time I knowingly used my weight as an involved middle-class white parent to intervene for my own child.

To this day, I have mixed feelings about my intervention. I was thrilled to see Ben thrive in his last year of elementary school, immersed in the theater projects his new teacher was known and loved for, challenged and motivated academically. Ben came home most days that year with a big smile and excited reports from the classroom.

And yet the question still lingered in my mind, What about the children left behind? Reminded of my father's admonishment about the paper left on the dining room floor that my siblings and I had all stepped over as children, I wondered, *Whose responsibility are they?*

I resolved to stay involved in the organizing that worked toward ensuring all children had effective teachers. I was to learn that this was one of the hardest challenges to address. What was an effective teacher, anyway? I could see that my definition wasn't always the same as other parents'. Some cared about creativity; others wanted no-nonsense rigor. We all wanted our children to learn, but learn what? And how?

This issue of the children left behind reared its ugly head in another way during Ben's last year in elementary school. John and I were notified that it was time for Ben to take the exam that would determine his eligibility to attend one of Boston's examination public high schools. We signed him up immediately.

In Boston, as in many other cities, some programs and schools are only open to students who pass competitive exams. Boston's Advanced Work Program started in fourth grade and fed into select middle schools and then into three exam high schools. The more rigorous academics offered to a student population that already demonstrated their ability to perform well was a contagious mix. While it tended to lift the academic performance of those students, it left the rest more isolated and with fewer resources.

It didn't seem right to me that the students who lagged academically then got less support, less rigor, and lower expectations than their peers. This was not a recipe for success—and it further intensified the divide created by the teacher "lobbying" we'd just addressed at the Trotter School.

Ben's best friend Ernesto did not take the exam. On one of my weekend stops at Ernesto's apartment I asked his mother, Judy, "You know it's time to sign the kids up for the exam school test. Why don't you register Ernesto?"

"Oh, that's not for him," she responded, and proceeded to explain that he was good with his hands, good at fixing things.

As a result of the exam school test, Ben went on to the school district's advanced work program for sixth grade and then to Boston Latin School, Boston's most elite public high school. Because he hadn't taken the exam, Ernesto moved from the Trotter to one of the worst middle schools in the city. His teachers quickly realized how smart he was and assigned him to help other students. Ben and Ernesto receded into different worlds, keeping in touch randomly through their teen years.

This situation highlighted a racial dynamic in the Boston Public Schools similar to many other schools across the country. The school system offered advanced work classes in some schools starting in fourth grade. These classes became the feeder system to prized seats at Boston's three public exam schools, where the best academic performers were invited to attend high school. Invitations to advanced work classes were sent out in third grade based on students' grades and standardized test scores.

The white, middle-class children in the system were typically more comfortable with the standardized tests than their counterparts of color. They were also aggressively supported academically by savvy, college-educated parents who understood how to get what they needed out of the system. As a result, they were disproportionately invited to the advance work classes. Parents were lured by smaller class sizes and more rigorous curriculum to leave the schools that didn't offer these classes.

Ben had been invited to advanced work class for fourth grade, but John and I had declined. It would have meant leaving the Trotter for a school that offered the advanced program, and we recognized the value of stability and community at the Trotter. Three years later, Jesse was also invited to advanced work class. Again, John and I declined. We saw no need to remove him from a school where he was happy, settled, and adequately challenged academically.

We also understood that our children's learning was about more than academics. Isolating them with other high achieving and mostly white, middle-class kids sent the wrong message. It told them in no uncertain terms that they "belonged" with the other white, middle-class children and that they were the smartest, the most likely to succeed. It also ignored the social development and other forms of intelligence that were just as important to our children and richer in a more diverse classroom. What if our schools put as much emphasis on compassion and social development as they did on academics? Wouldn't we be producing better citizens?

One day, years later, I sat in on a meeting called by an elementary school principal to convince parents not to leave his school for the advanced work program. Some of the parents understood the many benefits of keeping their children in the school. A few others treated the meeting as a bargaining opportunity.

"If you get rid of that art teacher, we might consider staying here."

"Bottom line, can you guarantee my son will still get into Boston Latin School if he stays here for fourth and fifth grade?"

I was horrified—not only at the level of self-serving manipulation but at the laser-like focus on academics.

What would this conversation look like if the parents whose children excelled socially talked this way?

"I don't want my Johnny in a classroom with kids who are so selfish. It would inhibit his social development."

"Jenny needs to be with other girls just like her to do her best. The less creative girls bring her down."

The mostly white, college-educated parents in that room would be incensed if the tables were turned in this way.

There has been much written about the narrowness of the ways in which our society has come to measure intelligence. Even Alfred Binet, one of the creators of the IQ test, never believed that intelligence could be quantified. The IQ test was originally developed for the French government for the sole purpose of identifying children with special needs in order to ensure appropriate schooling for them. Binet himself stated that the test "does not permit the measure of intelligence, because intellectual qualities are not superposable, and therefore cannot be measured as linear surfaces are measured." The creator of the SAT, Carl Brigham, disowned the test five years after he developed it for the military. By then, a number of Ivy League universities had begun to use it as part of their entrance criteria and never looked back.

The limitation of such standardized tests is that they only measure a very narrow range of intelligences. Well-known and widely respected psychologists from Harvard University's Howard Gardner to Robert Sternberg, past president of the American Psychological Association, agree that there are many definitions and types of intelligence. Our fixation on written tests that focus on reading, math, and logic provokes our educational systems to miss the gifts and potential of millions of children nationwide.

As the majority of white students in Boston moved into an advanced academic track, the students of color receded into less rigorous programs and less functional schools. And Boston's schools, like virtually every other public school system in the country, were disproportionately failing children of color. Less than ten years later, in 2000, black students like Ben's friend Ernesto made up 8 percent of students in gifted and talented programs across the United States, despite being 17 percent of the total school population. Similarly, Hispanic students made up less than 10 percent of gifted and talented programs, while comprising 16 percent of the total school population. Conversely, white students made up 74 percent of students in gifted and talented programs, while comprising 62 percent of the total U.S. school population. The convergence of poverty, racism, and narrow-minded measures of intelligence continued to lead to low expectations, lack of opportunity—and trajectories that perpetuate poverty, racism, and narrow-mindedness.

* * *

As Ben's elementary career wound down, the first economic downturn I experienced as a parent in the schools translated into deep budget cuts. In January 1992, rumors began to trickle out from Court Street. Ben was enjoying his final year at the top of the school pecking order, and Jesse was finding his rhythm as a second grader. Then parents got word that teachers were going to be laid off halfway through the school year.

It was bad enough that our children were in classes with thirty students when their suburban counterparts had twenty students to a class. We had learned early on that our bake sales and magazine sales and giftwrap sales were the only source of discretionary funds for field trips, theatrical performances, and literature for the classroom. Some years the fundraising had to pay for paper for the copy machine in the school office that cranked out reading assignments and chapters from social studies textbooks that were in short supply. Now, all of a sudden, the art teacher was being laid off.

One of those slips of paper endlessly coming home in my sons' backpacks arrived with a notice about a citywide parents' meeting.

"I won't be home for dinner next Tuesday," I once again announced to my family as we settled at the kitchen table over dinner. "You know that the art teacher got a layoff notice. And she's not the only one. Other teachers in other schools got laid off, too. Parents are meeting to figure out if we can do anything about it."

Ben and Jesse understood that the layoffs weren't fair to the kids or the teachers. Besides, they were growing accustomed to my near-weekly evening absences. A familiar mixture of guilt and righteous zeal passed through me. My own sons were doing fine. But that wasn't the point. Barely hidden below the surface of my dinner announcement, I was furious. I couldn't fathom how teachers could be laid off halfway through the school year. Didn't the school committee know how much money they had when they approved the budget for the year?

Natalie, Bob, Klare, and a handful of other parents coordinated our efforts through a series of evening phone calls. (This was before email.) We all became used to spending hours on the phone to each other after putting our children to bed. The Trotter contingent would be well represented at the citywide budget meeting.

On the appointed evening, I arrived at the designated school cafeteria to find it packed. Parents from across the city showed up, angry at the mid-year budget cuts and ready to take action. These parents came from neighborhoods I barely knew and schools I had never head of. They included African American, West Indian, Puerto Rican, and white parents, middle-class and working-class families, fathers and mothers and grandmothers. New names and faces swam through my mind as I tried to take it all in.

People were heated.

"We've had enough of this, year after year, and I'm personally fed up! This is not just about this winter's layoffs. We need to demand the budget that our schools need, and demand it NOW!" An African American man in jeans and a T-shirt stirred the crowd.

A murmur of agreement ran through the room.

A seasoned Latina organizer proposed that we develop a statement on what resources our children needed and deserved to ensure a quality education. Two dozen parents, black, Latino, and white, raised their hands to help out. Energized by the outrage and commitment that filled the room, I was one of them.

The smaller group met again the next week, still in a state of rage and indignation. A couple of parents of color I had met through the citywide parent council had stepped up to run the meeting. It was focused—unlike any of the previous citywide meetings I had attended.

"We can't just say that our schools need more money. More money for what?"

This is what we should be doing, I thought hopefully. *It's about time.*

The self-appointed group argued over words and ideas. The arts and music programs that were being cut were essential to a well-rounded education. Teachers could hardly be effective with thirty-five students in a classroom. Inadequate funding for textbooks and other supplies left teachers to pay out of their own pockets for the most basic of classroom supplies. The lack of full-day prekindergarten and kindergarten seats for all children meant those with the least support at home started out behind their peers by the time they entered first grade. The list of grievances went on.

Several meetings and statement drafts followed. The Parents' Agenda for Boston Public Schools eventually emerged, demanding guaranteed learning for all children. The specifics included smaller class size, strengthened multicultural education, improved special needs and bilingual education, more classroom supplies, increased early childhood programs, funded after-school programs, better maintained buildings, and expanded parent involvement. Our statement asked for parents to be recognized as full partners in their children's education.

Was this too much to expect?

With support from the teachers union, the citywide parent group organized a demonstration outside of the public library during Mayor Flynn's annual state of the city address. I invited people to my house to make signs for the big day. Children and parents and poster boards took over our dining room the evening before the event. Ben and Jesse helped make a placard that read, "STOP PLAYING POLITICS WITH OUR KIDS." I celebrated that I was contributing to something significant on a citywide level.

Ben and Jesse thought it was great fun as we carried our signs downtown on the subway. At each stop, a few more adults and children with signs got on. By the time we got to Copley Square, we were surrounded by a thick moving mass of adults and children and poster-board signs.

We arrived to a huge crowd surrounding the library. Adults and children of all ages and colors filled the sidewalks, chanting slogans at the top of their lungs. Five thousand teachers, parents, and students took part in the protest, with the Trotter well represented at over one hundred parents. I joined in the chanting. We were finally doing something big to address the problems in our schools.

Soon after our big rally, $6 million were restored to the school department budget.

After that first act of protest, I learned that the school department was the largest line item in the City of Boston's budget. And any time large amounts of tax dollars are at stake, decisions are going to be political.

The politics in this case had to do with who voted and who used the public schools. Ever since white families had moved out to the suburbs or shipped their children off to parochial schools en masse in the wake of court-ordered desegregation, the users of the system were predominantly families of color. Yet the voters of Boston for the next thirty years remained predominantly white. Fewer than 25 percent of Boston Public School students were white, while over 75 percent of Boston's white children attended private schools. It was not in the interest of the predominantly white voters of the city to fund the public schools.

The mayor, in deciding what level of city funds to allocate to the school department, was accountable to the voters, and the voters were not the families who used the schools. I was beginning to understand that "playing politics with our kids" was exactly what was going on.

* * *

Later that year, Ben started middle school. It was September 1992, and gang violence was continuing to heat up in pockets across the city. The Trotter School was the eye of the hurricane, calm inside as the Humboldt gang increasingly took over the surrounding streets. One sunny fall afternoon, a Trotter grandmother got caught in the cross fire of one of their never-ending turf disputes. As she walked her grandson home from school, a shot came out of nowhere, hitting her in the ankle. It was all over the evening news.

Klare and I knew the next parent meeting would be rough. This incident was so much bigger than us. That grandmother or her grandson could have been killed. The violence was closing in—way too close. We invited the police commissioner, city youth workers, and crisis intervention staff to the meeting. An unprecedented seventy-five parents showed up.

Klare opened the meeting, inviting the police commissioner to speak first. He thanked everybody for coming and went on to explain how he was stepping up police presence on Humboldt Avenue, now to include daytime hours. The police department was actively building profiles of the gang leaders with hopes of making successful arrests that would get them off the streets.

"Can your officers be here when school is getting out, at three o'clock?" one white parent asked.

"We'll do our best, ma'am."

The conversation then turned to the parents.

"I don't think the children should be let outside to play. It's just not safe—and so unpredictable!" one parent ventured.

"The kids need their exercise. We can't hold them hostage," another countered.

A few nods in the crowd signaled agreement.

By the end of the meeting, parents felt assured that a few new precautions were being put in place. But we all knew that there was nothing that could guarantee our children's safety. Random bullets knew no bounds.

Klare and I had done our best, and the rest was in fate's hands. A grim view, but I knew no other view to take.

Klare and I debriefed the following evening on the phone. She lived just a few blocks from the school and was as concerned for the neighborhood as she was for the school.

"Do you remember when school safety was first brought up at a parent council meeting?" she asked me. She went on to remind me about the direction the meetings had taken a couple years earlier. The parents who attended those meetings were only concerned with safety immediately around the school building and on the buses that took their children home. This narrow focus provided a stark example of what happened when we, the white, middle-class parents, ran the show. Klare was still smarting two years later.

The earlier group had completely ignored the need to address the violence outside the school building for the children who lived in the neighborhood. Seventy percent of the children in the school lived within walking distance, she reminded me.

"If I had been in charge, I would have assigned someone from the school to the neighborhood block watch effort immediately," she went on.

I was stung by her comment, unsure how to respond. I kept an uncomfortable silence, but I thought long and hard that night about the insight provided by her perspective. Scanning my memory of those earlier meetings, I had to concede that she was right. We had only focused on the buses and the school itself, not the neighborhood. I hadn't been in charge at the time, but that hardly let me off the hook.

White families continued to take their children out of the Trotter. I hung in, trying my best to explain to my kids where the violence came from. It was never easy.

"Mom, what makes people want to shoot and hurt each other like that?"

I never shied away from trying to explain complicated topics to Ben and Jesse. The answers to this one always seemed to fall short. I can't even remember what I said, perhaps because the emotion of what was surrounding us overwhelmed me during this period. I knew it was about racism. I probably talked about how generations of black people were blocked from living where they wanted or studying at good schools or getting good jobs. How so many generations of being kept back and in poverty made people want to explode. I doubt I used terms like "internalized oppression" that I was only just learning myself, how when everybody around you thinks you are going to amount to no good, you start to believe it yourself.

"Violence is never right, but people just lose control sometimes when they don't see anything positive or chances for success in their lives."

I didn't have answers that would make the problems go away, but I never gave a second thought to remaining in the public schools. My values were inextricably entwined with my commitment to public education. John and I knew many of our neighbors, both of us had jobs related to improving urban communities, and we were thoroughly settled in our now very comfortable house we had bought for $300 over a decade earlier. We never even discussed taking Ben and Jesse out of the Boston Public Schools. For all of our differences in upbringing, both John's and my families lived their values in their everyday lives and had taught us each well.

As other white families bailed, I stepped up my involvement at the Trotter and in the neighborhood crime watch group on my street in Jamaica Plain.

Not all parents approached our school problems with such equanimity. As we wrestled with bureaucrats and politicians and school authorities, many of the active parents simply lost it. When it came time to meet with their child's principal or face off at a school committee meeting, they shouted with rage at the injustice. Too many things were wrong in our schools, and too many people in positions of power seemed to be merely passing the buck. And these same people couldn't understand why we parents so often came across as hysterical. They dismissed the angry parents as just plain crazy.

Parents who used and supported big-city public schools had the paradoxical task of simultaneously defending from without and challenging from within a too-often dysfunctional institution. Even under the best of circumstances, this was a complicated dance.

In the fall of 1992, a new teachers union contract was being negotiated in Boston. A few of us parents—black, white, and Latino—who knew each other from citywide organizing decided to weigh in. None of us were against teachers getting a decent raise and benefits. We were concerned, however, that there were too many teachers who were not doing their jobs effectively and too many contract provisions that protected them.

I approached this campaign with some trepidation. My father and his father before him had been union organizers. The weight of their commitment pressed on me as we attempted to maneuver the treacherous waters between workers and management. The teachers union was quick to label any criticism as anti-union teacher bashing.

A group of us met to study the contract. We sifted through the compact little book designed to fit into a teacher's back pocket, and we found provisions that we agreed were not in the best interest of parents. Teachers were only required to work one evening per school year, usually the fall open house. Other than that, there was no requirement for parent contact. Dismissal of a poorly performing teacher required a series of elaborate steps over many months, any one of which implemented improperly sent the process back to square one. No wonder bad teachers were routinely bumped "up" to positions at Court Street rather than let go.

Our small band of parents formulated our position and took it back to the citywide parent council board. They readily added their stamp of approval. The day of the contract vote was looming, and I signed on to be one of the speakers for our group at the school committee meeting.

Hundreds of teachers had arrived before us, packing the school committee meeting chambers. Signs filled the room: "Renew our contract now" and "Vote yes for teachers." One of the first teachers signed up to speak during public comment made her position clear.

"You could pay us as much as Roger Clemens, and it wouldn't begin to compensate us for everything we go through!"

This was around the time when Roger Clemens, the then-darling of the Boston Red Sox, had just negotiated an unheard-of $5 million contract. That teacher's opening line summed up the prevailing sentiment of teachers. I quickly did the math—five million times four thousand teachers—that would be $20 billion. And it struck me that we needed another way to give teachers the support, respect, and encouragement they craved.

"Susan Naimark." Now it was my turn to go up to the microphone. The crowd of angry teachers scared the hell out of me. I was sure I'd get beaten to a pulp after stating the parents' position on their pending contract. I also knew that what we were asking for was the right thing for improving parents' relationship to the schools. I made my way to the table in the front of the room.

To my own surprise, my voice came out strong and steady. The script in my hand shook uncontrollably. As soon as I got my first few lines out, the booing started. It then grew louder, until one of the committee members admonished the crowd to let me be heard. He then asked me a question or two, the specifics of which I have no recollection. I could feel the heat of hundreds of angry teachers at my back. I finished reading my statement and gingerly made my way back into the crowd, looking straight ahead, my face flushed. Threatening murmurs closed in around me. When I got back to the spot where I had been standing, a teacher touched my arm and said, "It's okay."

School committee members then began to state their respective positions on the impending contract vote. The temperature continued to rise in the crowded room, teachers shouting and shaking their signs. One committee member was on the fence, the same one who quizzed me during my testimony. He then proceeded to cast the deciding vote, sending the union contract back to the negotiating table.

What had I just done?

This was a watershed moment for me. It was not only that I could see hard evidence that my activism was making a difference, although this was important. The jeering crowd had tested my mettle, and I had held up under the pressure. I had never before been the object of mob aggression. It was terrifying, but I hadn't been terrified. My clarity of conviction had overridden my tendency to avoid confrontation, at least in that one moment. And it felt good—really good.

The contract that was eventually approved included new provisions for parent contact. It increased the required evening meetings between teachers and parents from one a year to two. It also required that teachers post regular times each week they would be available to talk with parents. Inch by inch, we were increasing the responsiveness of the system to parents. We hoped.

CHAPTER FIVE

Bigger Stages,
Tougher Challenges

IN THE FALL OF 1992, reflecting on the successful budget and contract battles, I found myself wanting more. I was beginning to see how parents at one school got organized and the music teacher was reinstated, but another position at some other school quietly got cut to make up the difference. Trotter parents got bus monitors put on our children's buses, but that meant the monitors were pulled off some other route. This approach did not lead to equity and, altruism aside, we parents never knew which schools our own children might end up at next.

I ventured back to the citywide parent council and offered myself for its board of directors, not without some trepidation. As many as a hundred new parents came to the organization's first meeting of the school year and never returned. It didn't take more than showing up to get on the council's board of directors.

The organization's office had been moved to yet another leftover school space allocated by the central administration. The basement office at Boston Latin Academy was furnished in mismatched metal desks and tables provided by the school department. Heavy metal grates on the outside of the windows covered dingy gray windowpanes. A feeling of depression pervaded our board meetings.

The core group included grandparents raising their grandchildren, mothers on welfare, immigrant fathers from the Caribbean and Asia, a truck driver, a union organizer, a nurse, a lawyer, and a scientist, from neighborhoods across the city and countries across the globe. We all showed up more or less regularly because we cared. We wanted desperately to make the schools work better.

By the time I got onto the board of directors, the organization was down to three staff attempting to serve tens of thousands of families. The court mandate for parent involvement was still in effect, but the funding to encourage and sustain it was long gone. The director, Bessie, an African American woman who had devoted a good part of her adult life to this organization, carried a perpetually old and tired look, earned from years in the trenches as a parent, grandparent, and parent advocate. Soft-spoken yet firm in her convictions, she persisted in her work with a resigned, don't-bother-me-anymore demeanor.

I dragged myself to these dreary evening meetings after a long day of work and maybe or maybe not having eaten something since morning. A couple of parents worked night shifts, and these meetings were the beginning of their workday. How to focus our meetings was a thousand-piece puzzle. Do we start with the school department budget, which was never adequate to cover even the basics? With the administrators who talked down to parents or the custodians who hid in their supply closets watching TV for the better part of their work shifts? With safety on the buses?

My attention faded listening to predictable monologues. We were unable to direct our collective energy toward anything in particular. The multitude of individual acts of mistreatment were all likely true, but where to begin?

The meetings were only marginally managed by the chair of the board. Conversations rambled on without focus, regularly straying into random subjects until the vacant faces around the table told us it was time to go home. Staff seemed to focus their time and energy on individual parent intervention, not on organizing parents around shared issues. They left the board to its own devices. Under such conditions, not much was accomplished.

By the end of my first school year on the citywide council board, I had had enough. My success at standing up to a room full of angry teachers had given me courage. I wanted badly for this organization to be more effective. I equally wanted to maintain my integrity by bringing my concerns directly and honestly to Bessie, the director.

The last thing I wanted was to be called racist for challenging the director's long-standing ways of doing business. I couldn't unravel whether my differences with her *were* racist. At the time, I thought I knew what was right in order for the organization to have a greater impact. It hadn't yet occurred to me that "right" wasn't a simple, single way of looking at the organization or that my version of "right" was in fact subjective. I was lost in the notion that my college-educated, white, middle-class view of the proper way to run this organization was objectively correct. Now I can venture that my analysis was race-based, in the sense that it is typical, mainstream, white thinking to believe that there is only one right way to solve a problem. I don't think I understood that there might be many equally valid ways to understand the problems we were experiencing with the organization.

I knew that my challenge to Bessie's leadership could be seen as dismissive of her perspective. I approached this challenge warily, aware that a confrontation could easily be perceived as racially motivated. It would be easy for her to rally her friends, most of whom were black, to her defense. Were our differences really about race? I somehow knew they were, but couldn't yet articulate how. At their core, I think now that they were about distrust, deeply embedded in my own largely unconscious racial training.

Bessie, much like me, did not verbalize her feelings, at least not to me. I phoned her to ask that we meet. She didn't return my call. I left another message. She agreed to a face-to-face meeting only, I suspected, because she could see I was not giving up. When the time came to sit in the office beside her desk, I struggled to find the words that would express my frustration without offending.

"Bessie, I know you and your staff work really hard. But I'm concerned that we're not focused enough to make a difference. We don't have enough staff to intervene with every individual parent problem you get called about. I think we need to find a way to use staff time to organize parents, not solve individual problems one at a time."

I have no idea if my discomfort showed or my words offended. All I know for sure is that, just below my veneer of calm self-assurance, I was terrified.

Bessie sighed. I can't remember the specifics of her response, but I do remember feeling that she didn't address any of the concerns I raised. After about fifteen minutes, she got up to answer a phone call, signaling the end of our meeting. As I mulled over our conversation later, I tried to second-guess what she was thinking. And I assumed the worst. I attributed thoughts and motives to her that were my own projections, my own racial paranoia and lack of understanding of her perspective.

She doesn't like me because I'm white.

She doesn't trust me.

I had no way to know what she really thought, and my assumptions of mutual distrust overrode any other possibility. Looking back, I can now see that she may have been just as uncomfortable as I was.

I had no vocabulary to acknowledge the power that came with my race and class. Since then, I have learned that this simple acknowledgment can break the ice and create an opening for authentic conversation about difficult racial interactions. All I knew at the time was that our aborted conversation was no way to move an organization.

As my confidence in my organizing abilities grew, however, so did my frustrations over our continued ineffectiveness. School budgets were being cut across the city, thousands of high school students were dropping out, and the organization couldn't state a position on the problems that swirled all around us. Our board meetings continued to lack direction or closure. My meeting with Bessie hadn't changed a thing about how the citywide council functioned.

In January 1993, I offered to become the white cochair of the organization's board, after confirming that Lorraine was willing to run for black cochair and Janet for Latino cochair. We had all had enough of the status quo. We easily won the board officer elections, taking over three out of the four cochair seats. Other board members were relieved that we had volunteered for the thankless task of chairing monthly meetings. We were hoping to create a critical mass in leadership to turn the organization around.

As new cochairs, Lorraine, Janet, and I put agendas together in advance of meetings and tried to create focus on the issues of the day. We also spent time talking with other board members one-on-one. I selectively spoke my mind to test people's reactions, avoiding the few board members who had longtime relationships with the director. "Don't you think we should be taking positions on issues? I really don't understand what Bessie does other than show up at other people's meetings and not say a word." When others agreed, I made a mental note.

"That meeting last night: Are you as frustrated as I am at how things are going?" I asked one board member.

"Are you kidding? This has been going on for years. I honestly don't know why I'm still here, except that I keep wishing we could make something happen." This was Patricia, an African American parent from Dorchester who had been on the board as long as I could remember.

I became more confident that several of the African American board members shared our frustrations. The organization still operated under the federal desegregation order that required a cochair seat representing each of the major racial groups: black, white, Hispanic, and Asian. Aside from the cochairs, the majority of the board was African American. Still unsure and sensitive about racial fault lines, I felt that we couldn't afford to have the organization fall apart with the African American board members siding unilaterally with the staff. The staff worked hard, attended lots of meetings, and responded as best as time allowed to individual parent problems that came their way. It wasn't difficult to sympathize with their situation.

The new board leadership needed validation that our concerns were not racially motivated. Boston was still, after all, a highly tribalized city, where many residents were quick to side with their own people on any issue of consequence.

As the school year edged toward spring, the organization's meager budget began to run out. Bessie's funding proposals to several local foundations had all been turned down. At our March meeting, she reported that she and one other staff person were prepared to stay on without pay. Board members listened patiently as she went on to report on how many parents the staff had assisted during the past month.

Steve ventured out first. "I realize that the individual parent intervention that staff does is important. But we'll never get to bigger system changes if we don't focus on mobilizing more people."

Bessie kept up her usual resigned look. "If that's what you all want to do, go ahead." She made no offer to reconsider how she spent her time as the director and one of only three paid staff.

Bob suggested the organization create a strategic plan. The committee he formed began to meet regularly, outside of regular board meetings. This could be our point of leverage, I speculated hopefully.

Meanwhile, the first rumblings of education reform were moving through the Massachusetts legislature. The newspapers regularly carried headlines about a renewed state commitment to public education and the concessions the state legislature was going to ask from local school districts in exchange for expanded school funding. New statewide testing was going to dictate whether graduating students were eligible to receive a diploma. New rules about school governance gave explicit powers, such as hiring and firing, to school district superintendents, taking them out of the hands of local school boards. At Trotter and citywide parent meetings, we began to speculate on the implications. We realized that everybody but parents was weighing in on the new state legislation. The teachers unions and business interests were well organized. We saw no evidence that a parent voice was in the mix. We believed that we were the one constituency who could fairly represent the needs and interests of our children.

As the state legislature debated changes to teacher hiring and whether the business community would support increased taxes, we wanted to be sure the new legislation would address quality education. This focus seemed to be getting lost in all the pushing and pulling of various other groups.

Lorraine and Bob, both on the citywide parent council board with me, agreed we had to do something. Bob was one of the few white parents from the Trotter who had ventured into the citywide organization. I was glad that Lorraine signed on, as she was a working-class parent of color and someone I could count on to represent a different slice of Boston. We didn't yet know how all of the proposed changes would affect our schools. We did know that we needed representation of parents with different perspectives and experiences.

Bob called a few friends he knew who were active in their suburban schools. Lorraine and I reached out to other Boston organizations we thought would be interested. We called a meeting in the spring of 1993.

Out of our first few meetings emerged the Massachusetts Community Coalition for Public Education. By May, the nascent organization had mobilized parents from forty communities across the state to attend press conferences at the State House, organize petition drives, write letters to the editor, and attend town meetings with legislators to support increased funding for our public schools.

This phase of organizing is a blur in my memory, layered as it was on top of my school and citywide organizing commitments. What I remember most clearly were my late-night drives to Winchester, a suburb north of Boston, after I put Ben and Jesse to bed in Jamaica Plain, to coordinate newsletter production with Sarah, another coalition organizer. Before email, we had to hand-deliver the newsletter copy back and forth.

Sleep? Who needed sleep? I was running on fumes.

The urban-suburban coalition was a delicate balancing act. We never talked about the huge discrepancies in quality of our respective schools, but instead focused on our shared concerns to preserve and improve public education for all. Our newsletters and gatherings ensured that parents understood and weighed in on the biggest policy change in decades related to the education of our children.

In June 1993, the Massachusetts legislature passed one of the first comprehensive education reform bills in the nation. We had rallied parents from dozens of communities across the state to weigh in on the need for increased public-school funding. We had helped defeat a proposal to allow state aid to private schools, and we had trained hundreds of parents to be advocates for public education.

* * *

I took a deep breath after the new state education legislation passed. A month later, I found myself alone in a hotel room I could barely afford, wondering what the hell I was doing in Washington, DC.

I had somehow heard about the National Coalition of Education Activists. Immediately attracted by the organization's explicit acknowledgement of the role racism played in the dysfunction of public schools, I signed up for its annual conference. I arranged time off from work and paid for a train ticket out of my own scarce funds. Arriving at the hotel, alone, hot, and tired, I watched my hopes momentarily crash. There was no welcome sign, no hint of a conference starting the next morning.

I checked into my room and collapsed.

After a good night's sleep, I pulled myself together and headed for the opening plenary session. Scanning the crowd of nearly two hundred strangers assured me that there was, indeed, a conference taking place. Name tags hinted at a strong mix of teachers, school administrators, parents, and other school activists. The faces included an equally diverse racial mix. Okay, I knew nothing about the organization, but the crowd appeared legitimate. A glimmer of renewed energy surged through my tired soul.

That morning, the words of the keynote speaker, Senator Paul Wellstone of Minnesota, increased the voltage.

"We cannot decontextualize what happens in the classroom from what happens at home and in the community before and after school."

A national leader had just affirmed the framework of my activism. This idea, while not complicated, had been coming together in a less articulated form in my mind for the past ten years. This organization I had never heard of before that summer instantly earned my confidence.

NCEA had a practice of holding racial caucuses as part of their conferences, in which people met with others of their own racial group for discussion. The premise was that there are issues people are more comfortable sorting out with others like themselves, and that the insights gained were important to our work to improve our schools. That first year I showed up, there were caucuses for African Americans and Latinos, Asian Pacific Islanders and Native Americans.

Seeing no group that I could participate in, I naively hung a sign in an empty room for a white caucus. I needed somewhere to go for an hour, and that seemed the logical place if people were dividing up by their racial identities.

At the appointed time, I grabbed a chair up front in the empty room and waited. The room gradually filled until it was standing room only. I had no idea what to do, and there I was up front. I introduced myself and explained how I had come to hang the sign for a white caucus. I had never attended, let alone run, a white caucus in my life.

"What do you want to talk about?" I asked.

It turned out that we had a lot to talk about. White teachers in urban schools revealed their pain and exhaustion from trying to build respectful relationships with families of color who were hostile toward them. White teachers in predominantly white schools risked their jobs if they taught their students about racism. White parents like me were disturbed at our overrepresentation in parent organizations in schools that were majority families of color. Boston was not alone.

And neither was I.

The dam burst and the discharge poured out in that small room.

"I'm really not comfortable the way we white people dominate the agenda and decision making at my school, where we are obviously the minority."

"But what is our role, then? I want to be respectful, *and* I want to contribute."

"Can we be the bridge between white people and people of color? Someone needs to do it—my school is so divided right now."

"To be honest, I'd rather be seen hanging out with the teachers of color than the other white teachers."

"Isn't that patronizing to the teachers of color, really, like relying on their acceptance of us to be validated?"

"Bottom line, the trust just isn't there."

We didn't solve these problems in that first white caucus, but I immersed myself in the collective relief of voicing them out loud. We shared information on books and training resources and strategies that addressed white people's roles in challenging racism and better understanding the unearned benefits it affords us. Many of us couldn't get enough. We met in the hotel lobby after dinner. Our conversation continued well into the night.

A number of people of color at the conference came up to me afterwards and remarked, "It's about time you all realized you have something to talk about, too."

It had never occurred to me before this experience that racism was a *white* problem. As conference participants discussed the changes that were needed and analyzed who had the power to make change, I realized we all had important roles to play. White people had a responsibility, if we really cared about these issues, to use our power proactively.

This first step in solving the problems of racism—to name them—was simple enough. It just took me eight years to get there. And I learned that I could talk about race and racism without the roof falling in.

* * *

I returned to Boston three weeks after Boston city councilor Thomas Menino became acting mayor. I had gotten to know the man who was to become Boston's longest-serving mayor through a community organizing job I held that year in Roslindale, a Boston neighborhood where he was the district city councilor prior to becoming mayor. Earlier that year, for our first meeting together, in the community room of the public housing project where my office was located, Councilor Menino had arrived alone and relaxed—no fuss or fanfare, no aides trailing him as they did other city councilors.

I liked him immediately.

Our paths began to cross regularly. I appreciated his willingness to meet and engage everybody respectfully and as equals, whether they lived in the Archdale public housing projects or owned a business in Roslindale Square. He asked people what they thought, then listened. And he didn't have the arrogance that I never could stand in public officials.

Ray Flynn, his predecessor, had accepted an ambassadorship to the Vatican in July 1993, leaving the city's leadership in the hands of the president of the city council. Tom Menino had until fall to prove himself and gear up an election campaign to become the next full-term mayor.

I got my first call from the mayor's office as I was packing for our annual family vacation in New Hampshire. Acting Mayor Menino wanted my help on his educational platform.

Me?

I was stunned and speechless and not about to say no.

This was my first taste of having a direct line to someone who was in a position to really do something about the schools. Flattered and intimidated that he had invited me to work on educational issues for his campaign, I lay awake in the New Hampshire nights of our family vacation, listening to the crickets. Improbable thoughts rolled around inside my head. I had never before allowed myself to think so big, as in, "If I ran the schools, this is what I would do. . . ." My thoughts kept defaulting to a well-practiced reactive mode. It came easy to be critical of other people's decisions. But what would I do if I controlled the purse strings?

While picking blueberries along the edge of the lake, I slowly began to articulate a platform. The first draft the mayor sent me, written by somebody else, focused on closing down failing schools. I knew that this alone would not get our school system to where it needed to be.

I became a key player on Tom Menino's educational campaign team, inviting a few other parents I knew to the inner circle. I wanted to get parents of color to the mayor's table, grassroots activists who were strategic thinkers and committed to the public schools. This was the sort of role we had talked about at the NCEA conference, where white people with political access use it to bring in the voices of people of color who don't. We met a few times after I returned to Boston from New Hampshire, in a small meeting room in the mayor's office in city hall.

The first time I went to his office, Mayor Menino's face slid into a sly smile. "Want to see the secret elevator? I bet you didn't know about this, huh? It's the way the mayor can sneak out the back door with nobody seeing him." I never did see him sneak out the back door, and found his continued humility refreshing. When I asked him a year or two later how he liked being mayor, he offered that the part he liked best was being out in the neighborhoods meeting with community residents.

Tom Menino's educational plan took shape. The schools needed to reach out to community organizations and parents, treat everybody as partners. We highlighted the value of rewarding and replicating what worked, and the need for school-based management to be taken seriously rather than being treated as a perfunctory rubber stamp. His plan talked about expansion of full-day kindergarten and school-based after-school programs, about ensuring a welcoming atmosphere to parents through annual parent orientations like those I had been organizing at the Trotter for years. His platform drew from the parent statement that had been so well articulated only two years earlier.

This was how policy should be made, I thought: *with input from those most affected.* I remembered back to how the citywide group of parents had hammered out our shared beliefs, values, and priorities. The wisdom of that group did not require a college degree or election to public office—just a diversity of lived experience and willingness to stay in the room together.

It was heady stuff for me to see our ideas incorporated into real policy proposals.

"I want the voters to judge me on my progress with improving the Boston Public Schools," Acting Mayor Menino repeated at campaign stops across the city.

I could barely believe what I was hearing. Here was the first mayor in my experience as a Boston parent who seemed to want to make the schools work. He had taken a public stand early on that the schools needed fundamental change and that this change was critical to a vibrant city.

* * *

That fall, my one-year term as cochair of the citywide parent council board ended. Bob agreed to step up to take my place as white cochair. We were slowly orchestrating a coup, and the standoff was drawing near. Bob's strategic planning committee brought a proposal to the board for reorganization. With new functions and focus, it included new staff positions and job descriptions that better fit the new plan.

At the next board meeting, we forced a vote on whether the two remaining staff would have to reapply for their positions. People showed up for the meeting who hadn't been there in years. They weren't legitimate board members, but nobody challenged that. We usually accepted whoever showed up at meetings, whether they were elected through the formal annual process or not. Several of Bessie's friends showed up.

Bob called the vote to adopt the new strategic plan. All were in favor. Then came the follow-up vote, that all staff reapply for positions under the new plan. Bessie's friends raised their hands to oppose the vote. And I watched our plan unravel across that dreary conference room table.

As badly as I wanted the organization to change, I was still too intimidated by Bessie to challenge the votes of her friends. We had created a work plan but had no staff buy-in to implement it. The board could only go so far.

In retrospect, I can see that some of us board members didn't show a lot of respect for the staff. They worked long hours, and all they heard was criticism. I always felt that the director didn't respect the board or want to take any direction from us. With the clarity of distance, I can see why.

I found it ironic that the organization established to address racial equity had no mechanism to talk about race. To my mind, we were stuck in racial gridlock. There was a significant racial fault line to our differences, and I never heard anyone name it out loud.

After our failed attempt to reorganize the citywide parent council, my attention turned once again to the Trotter School. I resigned from the citywide council board of directors in January 1994. That fall, I threw my name in the hat for election to one of the parent representative positions on the Trotter School Site Council. This was the seat of power, where parent and teacher representatives met together to make school policy. I won the election and added one more monthly meeting to my schedule to replace the one I had dropped only a few months earlier.

I arrived at my second meeting of the School Site Council in October 1994, tired as usual and gathering energy from some unknown source for my second shift. I had just started a new job, with YouthBuild USA, a national youth development program. My work now took me out of town at least once a month, further complicating the family juggling act.

Ms. Leonard handed out the school's standardized test score data, disaggregated by race. Grade by grade, the black and Latino student scores were literally half the median scores of the few white and Asian students in the school starting at third grade. This was the first time I had ever seen school-wide test scores.

These were children I knew. No way were these black and Latino kids any less smart than their white and Asian classmates. Half as smart? The test scores did not match reality.

The teachers and parents of the site council sat around the table in the small meeting room adjacent to the principal's office looking over Ms. Leonard's handouts. Nobody said a word. In my mind, a parent of color should raise this concern. I held back until I couldn't stand it any longer.

"I don't understand how the black and Latino students test scores can be half the average of white and Asian students."

Ms. Leonard patiently laid out the range of factors that affect test scores: school readiness; bias in test content toward white, middle-class experiences; anxiety about testing.... And I learned that raising these questions was as much my responsibility as anybody else's.

Later, reflecting on the meeting, I was both puzzled and humbled by the thought process that led me to believe I *shouldn't* raise this issue. It was a sobering lesson in the frequently unconscious ways we feel responsible for people "like us" but not for "them," people we think of as unlike us. When I finally raised the question, everybody in the room moved closer to a shared understanding of the challenges facing our school.

* * *

The societal divisions between "us" and "them" came into stark contrast the following fall, when Ben and his childhood friend Ernesto entered ninth grade. In the fall of 1995, Ernesto started high school at Madison Park, Boston's vocational-technical school. Despite its lofty aspirations to train students for skilled technical careers, it was one of the lowest performing high schools in the city. That same year, Ben entered ninth grade at Boston Latin School, the city's elite exam school.

When Ernesto told the principal at his middle school that he was going to Madison Park, the principal's response was "Why?" Ernesto had been president of the student council. He had played a musical instrument and gotten active in the middle school's nascent theatre program, helping lay the groundwork for significant expansion of music and theatre programming at the school. During his middle school years, he had retrieved a set of Shakespeare books from the trash and read them all. He was a star student with no ready answer to the principal's simple question.

Ben had entered Boston Latin School two years earlier. All three of Boston's exam high schools started in seventh grade, while all the other high schools started in ninth grade—one more structure that ensured a widening rift between "us" and "them."

When Ben first entered Boston Latin School at seventh grade, our family's public school experience had taken on new meaning. The jewel of the school system, Boston Latin siphoned the highest performing students from across the city, including a high percentage of students from private schools.

An invitation to an open house for new students had arrived in the mail a few weeks before the start of Ben's first year at Boston Latin. Ben and I went. In the cafeteria, school staff milled around with incoming families. The headmaster congratulated our sons and daughters on their brilliant academic futures and presented a brief history of the oldest public school in the country. He went on to list the freshmen, junior varsity, and varsity teams offered in all the seasonal sports.

My thoughts drifted to the raggedy uniforms and equipment that English High School in Jamaica Plain used for a single varsity basketball team. The inequities made my head seethe.

On top of its sports teams, Boston Latin had five fully equipped bands, four orchestras, and five choirs. Alumni provided the financial support for an array of sports and music programs that rivaled the offerings of elite private schools.

The expectations were high (brutally high, some would say) and the atmosphere rarefied—not a word I would ever up until that point have associated with the Boston Public Schools. Families from the suburbs were known to use false addresses so their children could attend Boston Latin. Nowhere else were suburban families going to such lengths to get into the public schools of Boston.

I couldn't believe how white the crowd was. *Pinch me so I wake up from this fantasy. Could I still be in a Boston Public School?* Many of the mothers wore pearls, the fathers, suits. Where were all the families I had known from the Trotter? From the citywide parent council? This crowd did not look like the city I had come to know through my involvement with other parents across Boston's schools. As the group was ushered from the cafeteria to the auditorium, I could barely contain my tears of outrage at the stark differences in options available to children in Boston.

My head tilted skyward to take in the auditorium's high walls, lined along the top with the inscribed names of the school's illustrious graduates: Benjamin Franklin, John Hancock, Ralph Waldo Emerson, Leonard Bernstein. Ben's math teacher ceremoniously informed the group that Boston Latin was the best-endowed public school in the country.

On the way home from orientation I asked Ben how he felt about this, along with the long list of famous alumni whose presence he was about to enter.

"Privileged," he answered. Pausing for a moment, he added, "and lucky."

And I thought, what a fitting analysis of what it takes to get into a place like Boston Latin School: privilege and luck.

CHAPTER SIX

Me, a Public Official?

"WELL, YOU KNOW, YOU AREN'T EXACTLY AT THE TOP OF THE FOOD CHAIN."

Leave it to your children to speak truth to power. I don't remember exactly what the conversation was about, but I do remember very clearly Jesse's teenage response. It was 1997, and I was now on the Boston School Committee, with an expectation that I should be able to *fix* things. I was not ready to admit to myself how little control I really had.

The Boston School Committee membership had switched from elected positions to appointed ones in 1991. This was a controversial change, particularly in the black community, where people were loath to give up voting rights for which they had fought so hard.

My experience from years of attending school committee meetings for the Trotter and citywide parent organizations left me with a different analysis. The majority of the elected school committee members we faced off with barely paid attention to the issues on their agenda. Most served a term or two and moved on to higher office. The members of school committee in those years did not represent the families served by the Boston Public Schools. Too many of them were white, male, and far removed from the schools. The predominantly white voters of Boston elected school committee members, and the vast majority of white families were still, since court-ordered desegregation, not sending their children to the public schools. Neither these voters nor the committee members they voted into office had much attachment to the success of the Boston Public Schools.

The elected school committee wasn't much more than a political stepping stone, an easy entry into the world of politics still very much dominated by Boston's old-boy Irish network. The appointed school committee did not appear to have these aspirations. Their meeting agendas centered on education policy, and their discussions were more focused than those of the elected body I had observed.

When I first applied for consideration to be on the appointed school committee in 1991, seven-year-old Jesse said, "I hope you win!" His confidence in me was heartening, but it didn't get me appointed that first time around, or the second time a couple years later.

When I submitted my application for the Boston School Committee for the third time, in the fall of 1996, I realized I had a chance this time. Tom Menino was mayor, and he made school committee appointments. I was hopeful—and terrified that I might move to the other side of the battlefield I had fought on for the past decade.

While my application was pending, I drove to the Quincy Elementary School to observe a school committee meeting. I hung back in the auditorium to take in the scene. Seven committee members sat at a long table on the stage, with the superintendent seated in the middle, a black engraved nameplate and microphone poised in front of each person.

From the back of the room, I caught glimpses of two white men and two African American men in suits and ties, a white middle-aged woman in a slightly less formal knit suit, an older African American woman, and a Latino man dressed somewhat more casually. They sat impassively as the superintendent read a prepared report into his microphone.

I scanned the audience, trying to imagine myself on the stage in front of a hundred people—*these* hundred people. The image was too big to hold on to. I knew how to speak up during public comment and was an experienced spectator. But on stage with the spotlights in my eyes? I couldn't see it.

I don't remember anything of the agenda of that day. I do remember wondering incredulously, "That could be me up there." The idea made my skin tingle, my scalp crawl, in a mix of excitement and terror. It was an awful lot of attention. I left quickly and quietly before the meeting ended, wondering if I were ready for such a move.

My older son, Ben, was now taller than I was. Jesse had completed a thoroughly mediocre year of middle school and had, so far, survived his first two marking periods at Boston Latin School. With both sons now at Boston Latin, I worried that my sense of urgency around school issues would dissipate. Not that things were perfect there, but the stars were no longer aligned against academic success. The school's multimillion dollar endowment, wide range of sports and music and course offerings, and high academic standards provided supports and incentives that were virtually nonexistent in every other Boston high school.

Both Ben and Jesse had grown accustomed to me being out at evening meetings every week, working with other parents to make their schools more responsive, more accountable, more hospitable. They were teenagers and, luckily for me, not particularly rebellious ones; the pressures of parenting were beginning to ease up. They both had jobs and active social lives. I had time to myself again, in increments of an hour or two, as often as once a week. I sometimes didn't know what to do with myself, suddenly confronted with a small window of free time.

We held a family meeting after dinner one night about my school committee application. As we sat around the kitchen table, I warned everybody, "You know, if I'm appointed, I'll be home even less."

John, Ben, and Jesse were unanimously excited and proud.

"Go for it!" they all agreed.

John said nothing about the widening breach in our relationship, the tensions created by my physical and emotional absences from family life. If he had any reservations about the further deterioration of our marriage, he kept them to himself.

As December drew to a close, I watched the first snowfall of the winter out my window one afternoon at work. Rain suddenly turned white, then thick, then began sticking to the ground, the trees, the cars and street signs. I left my office and walked to the subway. The city had the fairytale look that comes with a bright, clean coat of freshly fallen snow.

Like the rain that had turned to snow that day, I was gathering my internal forces to prepare for the possibility of transformation. I didn't sleep well that night, alert with not knowing. Getting appointed to school committee was a big deal, and I was lost in limbo. Poised for action, or maybe not?

That week, my heart jumped every time the phone rang. I knew the decision had to be made before the month was out. I got the call from the mayor on December 28.

"This is a day you will rue for a long time" were Mayor Menino's first words over my telephone.

He offered me the school committee position, no stipulations or strings attached.

"I know you're going to do a great job."

Wow.

I couldn't believe this was really happening to me. As much as I had invested in the schools, it still didn't seem possible.

Me, a public official?

It didn't square up in the least with my self-image. For all of my boldness in taking on the issues I cared so deeply about, in my mind's eye I was still a quiet kid from a very white midwestern suburb. The one who was picked near the end of the line for games during gym class. Maybe even an imposter, doing a good job of getting everybody else to believe I was this *other* person who stood up and fought hard.

Besides, I hadn't grown up around powerful people. Power was something that always seemed to happen somewhere else. What did it mean to hold power? I wasn't sure that I knew.

Yet I had invested over a decade of my life in working with other parents to improve the schools. I had given up my evenings to school meetings, served as cochair of the citywide parent council, and taken part in launching a statewide coalition and a new citywide parent organizing network. I had learned a lot and felt that a parent voice was sorely lacking in the halls of power where school policy was made. I was ready to put my energy into attempting to achieve a higher level of impact. I thought I was ready for the discomfort of crossing over to the inside.

If I succeeded, I would be the first parent activist on the appointed school committee. I understood that this would be a challenging and complicated responsibility: challenging because I'd be the only one who might be willing to reach out and make myself accessible to parents; complicated because I knew that as a white, college-educated parent, my experience and perspective were not the same as that of most parents who sent their children to the Boston Public Schools.

If I could get on the inside, my role would be to kick open the doors a bit wider to let others in.

I phoned my doctor for guidance on how to keep myself healthy, sane, and energized. She recommended regular exercise, self-awareness, and a book about Buddhist meditation. I bought the book, tried to practice the long, deep breaths it described, and found myself hyperventilating.

My swearing-in took place in the mayor's office two days before the new year, on December 30, 1996. I arrived with my husband and two sons in tow, having convinced both Ben and Jesse to throw on button-down shirts and ironed pants even though it was school vacation. We found city hall quiet and nearly deserted for the holidays. The mayor's assistant ushered us into the inner office, where the city clerk laid open a huge leather-bound book on the table in the middle of the room. It was a low-key affair with my family and the mayor as witnesses.

"Do you solemnly swear to abide by the duties of your office and the laws of the Commonwealth of Massachusetts . . . ?"

Jesse heard me say yes and then quipped, "Mom, you've got to follow the speed limit now when you drive!"

I signed my name in the city register, and the mayor shook my hand.

Over the next week, dozens of calls and notes of congratulations and goodwill arrived in my mail. I couldn't help but notice, however, that they were mostly from white people I knew. It was a reminder that trust and support from the people of color I knew and had been working with were not going to come easy. I would have to earn them.

I also received my first weekly packet, delivered by courier to each committee member every Friday. I opened the big manila folder to find a VIP invitation to a corporate gala, invitations to school events across the city, news clippings from various educational publications, a couple of internal reports relevant to the next committee meeting, and a placard to put in my car window for use in the specially designated school committee parking spaces at school department headquarters downtown. This last item, in a city where downtown parking spaces went for $20 a day, said it all: you now have the keys to a very exclusive club.

If my children had not attended the Boston Public Schools, I could have easily been led to believe that the schools were fine and life was good.

So this is how it works. I had always wondered how public officials could sometimes be so out of touch with reality.

During my first week on school committee, one of the local evening newscasters invited me for an interview on his show. Nervous over this new level of attention, I asked John to tape the show. When I arrived home after the interview, I waited until after Ben and Jesse went to bed that night, embarrassed over what I was about to do.

I parked myself on our living room sofa in front of the TV, alone with a glass of wine, and turned on the tape. I listened and watched, several times over, analyzing my words, gestures, expression—wanting to understand my new public persona. I saw myself choose each word carefully, looking thoughtful and serious. My conclusion: I came across as knowledgeable and articulate but needed to loosen up and convey more of my passion for the issues. My nervousness didn't show through, but I could see how it inhibited my presentation.

The headline in the *Boston Globe* about my school committee appointment was smaller than I wished for, a one-paragraph news article buried on the inside of the City section. On the other hand, the *Jamaica Plain Gazette* ran a half-page profile.

The accolades sent my ego soaring. Then my first school committee meeting brought it back down to earth with an abrupt thud. My new colleagues welcomed me with polite nods as the chair called the meeting to order. I squinted into the bright lights, taking in the portraits of distinguished white men lining the walls of the committee meeting chamber. The agenda was perfunctory. The only audience members were senior-level school department staff keeping their ears to the ground.

How anticlimactic. I thought this was supposed to be a big deal.

When the meeting ended, one school committee member offered to take me out for a drink, interested enough to want to get to know me and talk about the agenda and challenges ahead of us. Other than that, I felt alone and on my own.

Ben, now in tenth grade, had developed a keen political sense—I had no idea where from. "Keep your enemies close" were his words of advice after that first committee meeting.

While I wasn't yet sure who my enemies might be, I phoned each of my new colleagues, leaving messages on voice mail and with assistants.

"This is Susan Naimark, your new school committee colleague. I'd like to meet up for coffee sometime. Give me a call and let me know when is good for you. Thanks."

My colleagues included a vice president at the Federal Reserve Bank, the head of a state agency, the president of a large human services agency, a retired community center leader, a university professor, and an activist in the Latino community. Ironically, because the committee was appointed, it was more racially diverse and more representative of various groups with an interest in the public schools than the elected committee had ever been. Its seven members included two African Americans, two Latinos, and three whites.

I methodically made my way through phone calls to my new colleagues. In most cases I didn't get past voice mail.

The first one I got on the phone begged off, congratulating me and explaining how busy he was. The next asked what I wanted to meet for.

"Just to get to know the other members, maybe a little better understanding of school committee."

We talked for a few minutes, mostly in generalities, and I thanked her for her time.

Bob, the school committee chair, offered to meet me for a quick cup of coffee downtown. A lawyer by training, he was at the time the head of a large state agency. An African American who had grown up in Boston, Bob was soft spoken and thoughtful. He didn't have much in the way of new insights to share, but at least he was willing to meet. He seemed harried. I didn't know exactly what to ask. It was all so new to me; I didn't know what I didn't know. I felt awkward taking up his time. After all, I had come to our shared role as a lowly parent. I still wasn't convinced I belonged as a peer with my new colleagues, with their important titles and credentials.

The one other white woman on the committee, Liz, also took me up on my request. She offered to meet me at a café near her home in the Back Bay, one of the most expensive neighborhoods of the city. She ran a large human service agency and was one of two committee members whose PhDs earned them the title of doctor. Her smile was stiff and her suit expensive. Again, I felt awkward and out of place.

The one member I knew a little before my appointment to school committee, Felix, Puerto Rican and a long-time community activist, confirmed that this was the extent of interaction between members.

How do they coordinate their work, compare notes, get to know each other? I wondered.

As it turned out, they didn't.

Only Bill, the white man who took me out for a drink after our first school committee meeting together, had gone out of his way to welcome me. He had been on the committee for a few years and was nearing retirement at his job at the community relations department of the Federal Reserve Bank of Boston. With his tweed suit jackets and tousled hair, he was one of the least forbidding of my new, mostly buttoned-down colleagues. I hung on to his kindness to reassure myself that I did, in fact, belong in this new role.

My name was added to the list painted on the glass wall beside the entrance to the school committee office on the sixth floor at Court Street. I went downtown to complete my official paperwork, pulling up to the parking spaces marked "School Committee Members Only" and slipping my parking permit in the front window of my car. Here on Court Street, I was now royalty.

The security guard barely looked up from behind his counter as I walked through the side entrance of the building. "You've got to sign in, ma'am."

I was relieved that he treated me like anybody else walking through the door.

As soon as I stepped out of the elevator on the sixth floor, however, that changed.

"Good morning, Ms. Naimark."

"Congratulations, Ms. Naimark."

"How are you this morning, Ms. Naimark?"

Who are all these people?

Perfect strangers smiled and acknowledged me as soon as I came into their view down the hall.

Am I supposed to know who they all are?

Overwhelmed at the idea, I sized up the sea of partitioned cubicles and offices surrounding me. This was only one floor of seven occupied by school department employees.

I gradually got to know my way around Court Street as I attended meetings with various staff. These central office administrators baffled me more than anything else I encountered as a new school committee member. I knew from my prior organizing work that poorly performing teachers throughout the system were routinely sent to downtown jobs. This was much easier than trying to get them dismissed. I also knew that the root cause of many of the problems we encountered at the schools—the late school buses, inadequate supplies, leaking roofs—resided at Court Street. These downtown administrators were the people who kept the system running, managing student assignment and transportation and textbook orders. After all my years of fighting the bureaucracy, I expected to at last see the dysfunction laid bare, up close.

Once I got there, however, I couldn't find the evidence.

The heads of the budget office, transportation, capital planning, and bilingual education all took turns reporting to school committee as items of relevance came onto our meeting agendas. One would appear with a pile of papers tucked under his arm and a small coterie of underlings trailing him into the committee meeting. Most spoke earnestly and looked tired. It didn't surprise me that they would ingratiate themselves to us, as they knew we would be voting on contracts and annual budgets and approving new policies.

While a few came across as incompetent, untrustworthy, or racist, I found the majority to be hardworking, well-meaning people. This puzzled me. I had expected to find evil lurking in every corner of the central office. How else to explain so many problems in our schools, so many children failing? The roots of the dysfunction did not become more obvious as I got to know the parts that made up the whole.

As I settled into my new role, I came to see that the institution had a life of its own. The school department culture sucked everybody in when they arrived and held them captive. Whether I stopped in at Court Street before work at eight in the morning, or for our committee meetings at six in the evening, many of the senior staff were in their offices working. Frequently, they headed back upstairs to their desks after our meeting ended at eight o'clock in the evening.

I wasn't always sure *what* kept them so busy, but it was obvious that most people at Court Street had no time to step back and look at the outcome of their efforts. They toiled away, working very long hours with limited evidence of the results. I didn't find the evil empire that I had imagined, the one that created so many barriers to parents getting their children's needs addressed.

One of my first actions after being sworn in was to send a letter to all 128 school parent councils offering to meet with them, update them on system-wide policy issues, and listen to their concerns. I knew from experience that most parents had little understanding of the connection between policy and practice. They also felt unheard and undervalued by the school system. This was a bold move I had been formulating once I got word of my appointment. When I suggested the idea to a few parent activists, they advised against it. Given the general malaise and distrust of parents, I did not expect to be overwhelmed by responses. I wanted to stake my space clearly. I overrode their counsel.

My two sons and a foster daughter had attended a total of 8 different schools, but these were hardly representative of all that I needed to know. I vowed to visit a new school every week, an ambitious but sincere commitment to learn as much as I could about the other 120 schools in the system.

I got a few calls and attended a few meetings as a result of my letter. The morning of the first of these meetings, I hovered in front of my bedroom closet, spending too much time trying to figure out what to wear. I was not ready to start wearing buttoned-down suits like other public officials I knew. My style up to this point had revolved around bargain-basement and thrift-shop scavenging. I now had an image to worry about. I was aware that I would be meeting many new people across the city for the first time. How to look appropriately respectful and authoritative, without being intimidating or stuffy? I still felt like one of them: a parent, a regular person. Not a "leader." While I hoped to become known for my actions and stand on issues, I did not want to be naïve about the fact that, at least in part, my credibility would rest on people's perceptions in these first encounters. I settled on tailored pants and jackets that weren't quite suits, colorful scarves, and my big gold hoop earrings. I bought a small spiral notebook and jotted down notes of what I would talk about and the issues on the school committee agenda that winter.

A couple of savvy headmasters intercepted my letters to their parent groups and invited me to their schools. I'm sure they were keen to get onto my radar screen. It never hurt to have a friend on school committee. I took the bait but arrived with antennae alert to the participation of parents, or lack thereof.

When I arrived on these visits, principals greeted me at the office door, offering a cup of coffee and steering me strategically through the school. They showed off the library and the new computer lab but stayed clear of the problem classrooms. In all my years as a parent, I was never offered a cup of coffee unless the parents were making it ourselves for our meetings.

One of these principals showed me around his school, more focused on *his* achievements than those of the students.

"Do you have an active parent council?" I asked casually. I wanted the truth, not what he could hear me wanting for an answer.

"Our parents don't really get involved in the school. . . ." His response was dismissive. I tucked it away for future reference.

Boston's schools had become more parent-friendly by this time, but not by much. Someone downtown had seen to it that all the schools posted signs at their front entrances that said "Welcome" above the name of the school. You could at least tell which door was the front entrance—a vast improvement from my first days of wandering the perimeter of the Trotter School, trying to figure out how to get inside.

When I got invitations to parent meetings, sometimes I went incognito. One evening, I slipped into the Hurley School in the South End, an elementary school two blocks from where I had lived when I first moved to Boston. The neighborhood was now on the edge of a new wave of gentrification. I was curious to see how it was doing in this new environment, who was attending the school, and whether it had attracted any of its new neighbors. I arrived at the 1950s-era brick building with heavy grates covering the windows, and allowed the school staff to welcome me as if I were a new parent. A few other parents stood in the lobby. We were led to the auditorium, where the guests left their coats on while the principal launched into her update.

"The P & D time this year has been reduced, and the WSIP will be reviewed at the next SSC meeting...." On and on the alphabet soup of acronyms went, incomprehensible to outsiders.

Any parent with any reservations about their ability to weigh in at their children's schools could easily be discouraged by such a welcome.

In May, five months into my school committee appointment, I got a call one evening from a member of an informal group of Jamaica Plain preschool parents. I had heard that such a group existed in my neighborhood, a middle-class, college-educated, group of white parents whose members rotated out every couple years as they shared extensive research and explored schooling options for their young children.

The woman on the other end of the phone line said they wanted to understand how school assignment worked in the Boston Public Schools. She invited me to an upcoming meeting at one member's home. While this group hardly fit the profile of other parent groups I had been meeting with in the schools, I agreed to join them. Everybody should be informed consumers, and I knew that Boston's assignment process was complicated.

I dutifully made copies of materials I now had easy access to as a school committee member, charts that listed all the elementary schools in the West Zone that these parents could choose from, indicating how many seats were available in each school and how many students applied for each seat. I arrived at the designated home that evening to a warm welcome from the host. A dozen parents sat casually around the living room.

As I passed around my handouts, I explained how the lottery process worked in making student assignments. I felt good about sharing this valuable information. They seemed to be pleased recipients.

Then I got to the part about what to do if you don't get your first- or second-choice school. I told them about Ben's first chaotic months at the Kennedy School and how the transfer lists worked, about the two different school-start times I was stuck with when Jesse started kindergarten in a different school from Ben. How I put seven-year-old Ben on the bus to the Trotter School at eight in the morning, then walked home from the bus stop with four-year-old Jesse and did laundry while we waited the extra hour to put him on his nine-o'clock bus to the Agassiz School. How I started dinner prep during this hour, in an attempt to recover the hour I lost after work since I now arrived at work late every morning after putting Jesse on his bus. How this happened because the "sibling preference" clause somehow didn't register with the computer when Jesse's school assignment was made that year.

"It wasn't ideal," I told the group, "but life isn't ideal. Sometimes you just have to roll with the punches. Besides, there's value for our kids in learning how to handle adversity, too."

That's when the meeting turned ugly.

"Are you trying to tell me that I should just stand by and watch my child be miserable?!" One parent practically jumped out of her chair, her voice high-pitched and anxious. Her previously mild demeanor dissolved before me, replaced by a righteous indignation that rose up through her shoulders and across her face. A few others shifted uncomfortably in their chairs.

I could see trouble coming. I took a deep breath, searching for the words that I knew she would not hear.

"It's not about standing by while our kids are miserable. It's about helping them figure out how to *not* be miserable when things don't go their way, which will inevitably happen at some point in their lives. I think children pick up on our anxiety as parents, and we teach them a lot when we make the best out of less than perfect circumstances."

Visions of spoiled children throwing temper tantrums on the grocery store floor flashed through my mind. I looked around to gauge the reactions of the rest of the group. The room grew quiet; people avoided eye contact.

I often felt inadequate at holding my own in an argument, and this interchange was no exception. The indignant mother didn't buy it. Our approaches were at odds. The conversation petered out, and the now-uneasy host escorted me to the front door.

I was never invited back to the parents' school research group in my neighborhood. And I made a mental note to focus my precious time on working with other parents who sorely needed this information. The school system had spent generations keeping black students and other students of color from getting equal access and equal resources. These students continued to be failed disproportionately by the system. I was now in a position to do my part to equalize the playing field.

I continued to make myself available to parent groups whenever I could, not withstanding my strained experience with the Jamaica Plain preschool parents. When I got a call inviting me to meet with a group of Spanish-speaking parents in East Boston, I readily accepted. This meeting was part of a workshop series organized by a local community organization to train immigrant parents to understand how the school system worked and their roles as parents in supporting their children's education. Their meeting took place in the Umana-Barnes Middle School library.

I pulled into the school parking lot as it was just getting dark. The dinner staple of community meetings, pizza and soft drinks, was already laid out on one of the Formica-topped tables off to the side from the large round tables set up for the meeting. About two dozen immigrant mothers sat at tables in small clusters, a few with children sitting beside them, talking to each other in Spanish. I knew from the demographics of East Boston that the majority came from Central America.

The parent organizer had worked with me in advance to develop my presentation in Spanish. She translated the simple flow chart I had created for parent meetings that showed what decisions are made at each level, from the school principal up to the school committee and the mayor. I nervously flipped through my notes as I was introduced.

The mothers patiently corrected my Spanish, staying with me through the entire presentation. What a relief. I was pleased that I could deliver my presentation in their native language, stretching the limits of my foreign-language skills.

The ensuing discussion was a sharp contrast to the Jamaica Plain preschool parents.

"I am so frustrated that I can't help my son with his homework," one mother lamented in Spanish. A number of others nodded their heads vigorously in agreement and jumped in with their own concerns about not understanding the math, science, or English lessons of their children. Many of these parents had been in the school system for a few years, their children in middle and high school. Most had no idea that each school was required to have a school site council that included parents and that had to sign off on the budget every year.

We brainstormed together about where they could look for after-school tutoring: the local library and community centers, ask the teachers or office staff.

"But nobody in the office at my son's school speaks Spanish. How do I even ask for a meeting?"

Parent sessions like this one affirmed why I got myself on the school committee. I left the Umana-Barnes Middle School that evening satisfied that I was doing the job I had set out to do. The children of these parents were our school system's anonymous statistics of failure: Latino teens whose families didn't speak English. Their parents were finally getting the information they needed to change that trajectory.

If the schools were intimidating to parents like those at the Umana-Barnes, their involvement at the policymaking level was even more of a stretch. School committee had a public comment period where anybody could sign up and speak for three minutes. We committee members sat at a long table on a raised platform in the front of the school committee chamber. The majority of people who attended these meetings were insiders of one sort or another: senior administrators who needed to keep themselves informed of new policy initiatives, education reporters for the local newspapers, a few tireless advocates and watchdog groups—all of whom knew each other.

There was nobody to welcome newcomers, nobody to offer translation in a system where over one-third of students did not speak English at home, nobody to point out where the agendas and other handouts could be found in the back corner of the room.

The school committee secretary set a timer when each person started to speak during public comment. Unless the speaker was practiced at preparing her remarks, she would be cut off with a loud *rrring*.

I watched from my seat on the platform in dread, waiting for the startled look on the face below when the timer rang, often bringing the speaker to an abrupt halt as she lost her train of thought. Protocol did not require or encourage committee members to respond to public comment. The interrupted speaker would look up across the platform at seven stony faces. Once I began to get comfortable in my school committee role, there were times when I couldn't hold my tongue, watching the agony of the speakers below me. At these times, I leaned into my microphone and offered a sympathetic response to a nervous parent who had made it this far to present her concerns.

"Ms. Naimark, I'd like to remind you that public comment is for the public. No responses, please." The chair had a way of keeping speakers at public comment in their bewildered place.

* * *

When I first started on school committee, I wondered if I could maintain the schedule. Between the TV interview, my first committee meeting, and other invitations, I was out at meetings four evenings during my first week. I barely saw my family, coming home hungry at nine or ten o'clock at night to find cold leftovers for dinner and Ben and Jesse finishing up homework, no longer waiting for my arrival. If I thought I was stretched thin before now, this new role quickly took my calendar to a new level of overbooked.

After my first few months, I got used to the grind. But by Friday evening, I was brain-dead. I arrived home from work, mechanically retrieving from the porch floor the thick manila envelope delivered from Court Street. I often stared blankly at it for a long minute, weighing its contents in my hand and wondering when I would find the time to read them.

I moved through the weekend like a robot, doing my Saturday chores, waiting for John to come home from work. I attempted to keep tabs on Ben and Jesse's now-teenage schedules, squeezing in conversations so I could catch up with their lives.

My biggest fears were that the basic management of our household would fall apart and that I would be unprepared for school committee. If I didn't keep on top of the bills and housecleaning and laundry every weekend, I was convinced it would all become rapidly and irrevocably out of control. Sunday morning, I finally opened the school committee packet.

If I let myself fall off the treadmill, I would never be able to get back up.

John alternated between supportive and resentful, warm and cold. I never knew which to expect when I arrived home, still flushed from the attention I was now receiving. One night he sat with me at the kitchen table as I ate my cold dinner, wanting to hear the details of my day. On another night he barely looked up from his desk, keeping his face and feelings hidden as he balanced the checkbook.

I took my doctor's orders seriously, going swimming early every morning of that first week at the municipal pool down the street from my home. Later on, I switched to jogging around Jamaica Pond, trading chlorine for fresh air. My predawn exercise provided the only reliable thirty minutes of peace and solitude where my thoughts were my own over the coming years.

On a good day—one with no breakfast meetings—John made the school lunches for Ben and Jesse, who headed out the door at seven o'clock to catch the bus to school. I left shortly afterward. My forty-minute subway ride to work allowed me to read through the news clippings that arrived in my weekly school committee packet. Hungry for understanding and any new ideas I could garner from the challenges and successes of other school systems across the country, I did my best to keep up with this reading. My briefcase became heavier by the week.

As the subway neared my stop, I made lists in my little notebook of the people I wanted to talk to about the issues of the day: individuals I respected who worked in advocacy organizations, parent groups and staff in the schools most affected, experts at local research or educational institutions. These phone calls—before cell phones—ate up my days, their weight on my time staggering. If there were five people I wanted to touch base with on any given issue, it could take up half a work day, or two or three evenings on the phone. If I didn't get home from evening meetings until nine o'clock, that didn't leave much time for calls. The simple math of it didn't fit the available time.

By the time I got off the subway for my day job at Davis Square, I had added sticky notes to a few news clippings and transferred them from the "reading" folder to the "follow up" folder tucked inside my briefcase. As I got on the elevator to my office, my day job would slowly click into view in my brain, on some days more successfully than others.

When issues on the school committee agenda got heated, my office phone rang off the hook. Or I spent hours tracking down people who might provide some insight on the topic at hand. Otherwise, my work for YouthBuild USA kept me moving all day.

My days went by in a blur. More often than not, I didn't take a break between my arrival at eight and departure at five thirty for school committee commitments. Some days, I realized as I left that I hadn't eaten all day. As I packed up to leave the office, I quickly scanned my calendar to remind myself where I was scheduled to be next, and took a deep breath. Time to switch gears and muster some hidden source of otherwise depleting energy.

My back and neck began to hurt. Even my religious exercise routine didn't loosen them up. My finely tuned schedule didn't have space for disabilities, no matter how minor or short-lived. I scheduled a doctor's appointment, arriving hopeful that she'd find the source of the problem. After the usual poking and prodding, the only problem my doctor could locate was tight neck and shoulder muscles, worse on my left side. I lifted myself off the exam table and picked up my briefcase to leave. She took one last look at me.

"Wait a minute. Can we put that briefcase on the scale?"

It weighed in at over ten pounds. Her face changed to a "what-were-you-*thinking*?" kind of look, and I started weeding out briefcase contents in my mind.

I traveled for work once or twice a month for meetings, visits to local programs we supported, or training workshops I organized and ran. I often wondered when John would grow tired of picking me up at the airport after missing me at home for days on end, an empty seat at the dinner table. I wondered when Ben and Jesse would push beyond our mutual joke that we got along well because I was not around to meddle in their lives like other mothers. What I didn't realize was that my returns home were not about picking up the pieces so much as about meeting the emotional needs of family life. This is much harder to negotiate than who takes the kids to the dentist.

Then, one morning in June 1997, I woke up and couldn't come up for air. I was drowning. I numbly dressed and walked to the subway. As soon as I arrived at work, I found myself in a co-worker's office, leaning against the closed door, sniffling and wiping tears from my eyes. I couldn't let on how hard a time I was having trying to juggle my day job, maintain any semblance of family life, and manage the sinkhole called school committee. Never mind time for myself or my marriage.

I was the one who always had to prove I could do the impossible. It started with little impossibles, but they kept getting bigger. Now they were truly insurmountable impossibles. I was teetering on the edge of losing myself to a total commitment to the cause of our schools—forget about my family, my marriage, or my personal needs, and go for maximum impact—or total breakdown.

I emailed my friend Beth, an elected school committee member in a nearby suburb whom I had gotten to know through our earlier statewide education organizing efforts. She tried her best to put some perspective on my distress.

"Of course you had a meltdown. You do not have a normal life," she reminded me. "These are not normal sorts of responsibilities where you can neatly compartmentalize, 'now I do school committee, and then I'll do my day job, and then I'll supervise a little homework.' . . . You can never leave school committee behind. Anytime you are out in the community, at the grocery, on the subway, someone wants to loudly, usually, tell you something that you cannot do anything about at that moment but which you cannot forget."

This was to become the first of several annual June meltdowns, when the school year wound down and just before school committee went on break for the summer, providing its members with a couple months of breathing space. I had come to understand, but only intellectually, that I would be able to achieve more if I took better care of myself. But I couldn't figure out how. I was functioning at 120 percent capacity and burning out the engines.

I hung on to my sanity in the most tenuous way during these meltdowns because I had "Mr. Mom" at home. When I had first started working at YouthBuild in 1994, John was able to shift his work hours so that he could be home by mid-afternoon. He helped with the homework, cooked the dinners, picked up the groceries, and otherwise enforced the rules of life with two teenage sons. The role reversal helped neutralize my resentment built up over the previous years, when I had carried the weight and responsibility for our home life. By the time I got on school committee, the teenage sons had learned not to expect much of me. I worried what price I would pay down the road for my extended absences. My home responsibilities were pared down to doing laundry, washing the kitchen floor, and organizing our social life, which was why we didn't have one.

Yet I couldn't see letting the summer go by without finding *something* to feel more optimistic about. I had survived my first six months on school committee. I now needed to take advantage of the summer downtime to take stock. On a hot July weekend, I invited Felix, one of my new school committee colleagues, to a cookout at my house.

Over the past several months, Felix had become my interpreter of the mysterious functioning of the school committee. We had also shared an ongoing conversation about how to better engage and inform the public of our work. Felix had become my partner-in-crime, the only other committee member who regularly spoke up during meetings and voted against the majority when necessary, on principle. Well-known in the Puerto Rican community, he took their concerns seriously as Latino failure rates began to surpass those of African American students.

Over barbequed chicken and a cold beer, we analyzed our shared frustration.

"Sure, there are problems we're not addressing. We need the public to also know there are many good things going on in our schools," Felix reasoned aloud.

I agreed with Felix. We had to find ways to turn around the poisonous culture of the school system, start reinforcing the positive. So we launched a weekly television show, *Let's Talk About Schools*, on the local cable access station.

That September, Felix and I went to orientation at the station. The program director showed us around the studio, described how to handle the speaker switch for phone call-ins during our live shows, and gave us worksheets with suggestions for how to script our half-hour show. The studio, with its potted-palm backdrop and bright lights, was to become my Monday evening home for the next seven years.

I started lists of people I felt were making good progress in our schools. My list was long and gave me great hope. I knew nothing about television production or hosting, but this was the community access station. The bar was low; we weren't expected to be professionals. Besides, I had control. I expected this new endeavor to be more fun and encouraging than many of my official school committee commitments.

Felix and I took turns hosting and inviting guests to cover various topics of relevance. School principals, teachers, youth organizers, and policy staff hidden away at school department headquarters were flattered when I sought them out to appear as guests. We wanted to get out a different story about the possibilities for change in the Boston Public Schools.

I focused my first show on family involvement, a topic close to my heart.

CHAPTER SEVEN

Lost in the Shuffle

ONE SATURDAY, I STRUCK UP A CONVERSATION WITH JESSE'S FRIEND Jared when he arrived at our house for the afternoon. Jared and Jesse had become friends in middle school, where they were both in the advanced work class for sixth grade. Jared was one of those kids whose minds were always working but who didn't apply themselves any more than required, and sometimes less, at school. The boys were now in ninth grade, Jesse at Boston Latin School and Jared at Hyde Park High School.

"Jared, how are things going at Hyde Park High?" I asked.

Now that I was on the Boston School Committee, getting this kind of on-the-ground intelligence was vital to my job.

Jared admitted that he had started to skip classes.

"My teachers are covering material I learned in seventh grade."

His mother found out when she got Jared's report card at the end of the marking period. She was furious that nobody called sooner to inform her of his regular absences.

"I was kind of waiting to see how long it would take for anybody to say something," he volunteered. Jared then went on to tell me about one teacher who selected a student each day to send out during class to get a cup of coffee.

"That doesn't sound good, Jared. What about your other classes?"

"Well, in math class we sold teddy bears last month. We were supposed to calculate the profit."

No wonder he was bored, I thought. *This sounds more like a fifth grade assignment than high school material!*

Luckily, Jared had a parent who noticed there was a problem and intervened. She threatened punishment if Jared didn't show up at school everyday. He got back on track, finishing high school with a diploma and a thoroughly mediocre education. But I knew that Boston's high schools were full of other students like Jared, many who weren't as fortunate to have a parent who jumped in to intervene in the shortcomings of their education.

That winter, as Jared cut classes and I eased into my second year as a public official, the school committee set up a high school task force with the Boston Teachers Union. The task force was charged to look at how to improve the district's woefully underperforming high schools. I ended up as the school committee representative on the task force when my colleague Bill got into a serious accident. Bill had been the only school committee member to reach out to me when I first was appointed. He had worked with school-to-career programs for years and was the committee's expert on high schools. He now lay in a coma that ultimately required many months of recovery and rehabilitation before he would be well again.

Bill's absence left a hole in the school committee. And I questioned my adequacy to fill his shoes. Sure, I was working with programs across the country that served high school dropouts. But he was an *expert*. I hadn't been at it for years the way he had.

Through the spring of 1998, the task force met at Boston Teachers Union headquarters, a nod to our shared commitment to finding solutions for Boston's high schools. The task force membership included a few high school teachers and administrators, senior school department staff, the teachers union president and high school liaison, representatives from community-based programs for teens, outside experts, and a couple of parents. The conference room where we met was brightly lit, its hard surfaces mirroring the feel of our meetings. We all knew that *something* had to change. What and how would be the points of contention.

National research pointed to small schools being better at keeping students from falling through the cracks. Jared was just one of hundreds of students in Boston at risk of failing in, or being failed by, our high schools. At the task force, the experts proposed breaking up our large high schools into smaller learning communities. We discussed underlying principles for whole school change, knowing that simply tweaking around the edges would not be enough.

The task force scheduled visits to almost every high school. We needed buy-in from teachers if we were to have any hope of making change. At each school, an announcement in the faculty bulletin invited staff to join us for a brief after-school meeting. Task force members introduced each session with a short presentation on why things needed to change and what our preliminary research was leading us to recommend. Then we'd open up for questions and discussion.

Sometimes there was lively discussion, but more often the staff sat sullenly in the school auditorium with their coats on, ready for a quick exit. At one such meeting, a young teacher approached me as we wound down the formal program.

"You know, if you really want to see anything change, you should renew the superintendent's contract right now. People in this building aren't going to budge if they see this as one more new initiative that will be over before it's started."

She was right. I brought this comment back to the school committee chair. This was probably not the first time such an idea had been brought to her attention. By the end of that year, we had extended the superintendent's contract, making him the longest standing superintendent in Boston in many decades and defying national statistics on big-city superintendents. As urban school districts across the country tried mightily to turn around rampant failure, the average tenure of their leaders was 2.5 years. Some aspects of change simply required leadership that hung in long enough to see them through.

But at the high school task force, resistance was building. One veteran teacher emailed me his reaction to the task force's work: "Out in 'District High Schoolland' the term 'whole school change' is being used by administrators as a threat to the faculty.... What is the purpose of the 'whole school change'? To cloud the issues?" He went on to refer to the entire proposed change process as "threat jargon." This teacher taught in a school where half of the students were dropping out between ninth and twelfth grade. His view of change as a threat sent chills through me. How did he expect the problems to be solved without *something* changing?

The school district hired a well-respected national consulting firm to do some research for the task force. As copies of the consultant's data report were passed around at a task force meeting, the room became quiet.

The researchers had sorted Boston's tenth grade student math test scores by teacher. These were all basic (not honors or accelerated) math classes in the district high schools, with comparable starting scores for each group of students. The sort found that roughly one-third of the teachers were able to move their students well beyond one year's worth of advancement. Another third demonstrated results that were roughly what should be expected in the course of a year of instruction. The final third group of teachers showed declines in student achievement for the students they taught, year after year.

This data paralleled system-wide findings that showed 95 percent of all high school students testing at the lowest level on state math tests. It reflected my own experience with a foster daughter John and I had taken in when Ben and Jesse were younger. She had received As and Bs in tenth grade math and lost a job because she couldn't do basic arithmetic. When I went to talk with her math teacher, he responded, "But what are you worried about? She's such a sweet kid." I was worried that she was going to complete high school without the basic skills to hold down even a minimum wage job.

The consultant walked the task force through the report findings. When she got to the data on tenth grade math teachers, the teachers union president's voice rose in the conference room that suddenly felt too small. He chastised the report's authors for the simple comparison of high school teachers that ignored so many other factors affecting student achievement.

"This data is misleading, and I don't want it to leave this room."

Other task force members disagreed.

The union president was not swayed. "I can tell you right now, if this data becomes public, the union is through with this task force."

He stood up and stormed out of the room, his high school liaison close behind.

To me, this data got to the heart of a problem we had tiptoed around for too long. I had heard too many stories like Jared's, particularly at the high school level, from my sons, their friends, other parents. Boston's teacher evaluation protocol, hammered out between union and management as part of contract negotiations, had evolved over many decades in response to biased principals and meddling school committee members. Each new iteration drove it closer to unworkability, as it specified under what conditions a principal could visit the classroom, in what form they needed to write up any concerns, and how many days before they could visit the classroom again.

For decades, a teacher had never been fired in Boston. That was changing under the current superintendent, Thomas Payzant, but slowly. I had heard rumors that the teachers union high school liaison had been counseling teachers how to get around the evaluation process. On one high school visit, the rumor was confirmed when a teacher came up to me for advice. He described how he was in the process of being evaluated out.

"The union told me the evaluation process has to start over if I go out on medical leave. Do you know any doctors you could recommend?"

Was he serious?

I puzzled over the entrenched resistance to change I kept bumping into among teachers, always strongest at the high school level. The year of our high school task force, a Harris poll found that a majority of teachers across the country believed parents took too little interest in their children's education. They also said that parents should not be actively consulted about subjects taught in the classroom. From all sides, the message from teachers was loud and clear: *Leave us alone, and stay out of our way.*

This flew in the face of everything I was learning in my day job and volunteer work about how to make change. We needed collaboration and buy-in.

I was beginning to see some of the factors behind this intense resistance. With high schools structured around forty-two-minute periods for each subject, it was impossible for teachers to build relationships with their students. Not only did they have to work with 100 to 150 students every week, but they only related to these students around a single subject. If a student struggled with math but loved music, how would a teacher know? They were unlikely to make connections that might make a subject come alive.

Giving useful feedback to students was even less possible. If a teacher spent even fifteen minutes each week providing feedback to each student, that would be twenty-five hours, on top of classroom prep, teaching, and homework review time. There was no way a teacher could give individual feedback to that many students in the course of a week.

On top of these obstacles, by high school most students had been sorted and sifted into ability groupings. The teachers who had the general or applied math classes got the message with each student roster that their students were not as "smart" as the students in Advanced Placement math. Students landed in these high- or low-ability groupings based on a lot of factors beyond their innate intelligence. But with tiered courses typical of most high schools, teachers too easily could predetermine the achievement of their students.

These structural biases of most high schools reinforced any other biases held by teachers. We all have biases. But when a teacher has little ability to get to know her students as individuals, and these students arrive at her classroom already labeled for success or failure, biases blossom. The black boy who triggered threatening stereotypes as an eight-year-old now triggers stronger stereotypes, as does the white boy or Latina girl or Asian girl. With Boston's teaching force still over 75 percent white, the gaps in understanding loomed large. And the stereotypes still alive and well in the larger society easily filled these gaps.

I searched for models for a different type of relationship between teachers, students, and families. I found part of the answer in my day job. YouthBuild worked with dropouts of school systems across the country. The program model included alternative education, job training, and leadership development components. Some of the local programs were more successful than others at bringing the disenfranchised youth of America back into the mainstream. Even so, these programs had success rates as good as or better than any other national program working with low-income, out-of-school youth. And all had more young people wanting to get in than funding could support.

Part of my job was bringing together staff and students from our programs to inform our national program standards. In spring 1998, in the midst of my assignment to the high school task force, I convened a meeting of program directors to get their input.

"There's no way we can expect these kids to get their GED in ten months. The majority of students in my program are coming in at a third grade reading level," reported the director of the local program in Phoenix, her cheeks flushed and jaw set. "You'd have to extend the program to at least two years to see that kind of progress, and my funding won't allow me to do that. A GED sounds good, but it's totally unrealistic!"

"But what does it mean for us, as a national program, when young people can say they've graduated and they haven't even earned their GED?" responded Erin, the director from Philadelphia, standing up and leaning into the table to emphasize her point. "We want this program to be credible, and there's no way that a bunch of graduates out there who don't have any academic credentials will create that credibility!"

Erin was the veteran, having founded one of the first, and most successful, programs in the country. Her program was also the largest, with 100 students. The school district of Philadelphia, from which her students had dropped out, was also one of the largest in the country, with 150,000 students. One day, Erin got a phone call from the district. "Can you take another 1,000 students in your program?"

When we heard this story, we all laughed until we cried. A central point of success in the YouthBuild model was the smaller program size that gave struggling students the attention they needed. Boston was clearly not alone in its challenges with large, failing high schools.

I watched the program directors from across the country engage in impassioned debate, honored that I worked for an organization that attracted such committed people. It was a stark contrast to the sullen teachers and harried principals I met in so many of Boston's high schools.

We had set aside the better part of a day to review student data from YouthBuild programs across the country and develop recommendations for attendance and graduation requirements. After much debate, the directors at the meeting proposed to issue certificates of completion to differentiate those students who did not attain their GED from those who would be called graduates. Local programs would be encouraged to find funding to keep students for two years instead of the standard program model that only paid for ten to twelve months. This would give more students the opportunity to earn their GED and the national graduation certificate.

Next, it was time to take the proposed standards to the national youth council.

The youth council meeting took place in Boston that summer. Another staff person and I gathered up the young people arriving at Logan Airport from Baltimore; Gary, Indiana; Atlanta; Portland, Maine; Brownsville, Texas; and other points across the country. Most were seasoned youth council members and knew the routine. They were well beyond those first airplane trips and the anxiety of leaving home for the first time.

At our previous meeting, I had spent time getting to know Nina, a tall, young, African American woman with the high energy particular to native New Yorkers. I pulled up to the train station excited at the prospect of reconnecting. Nina emerged from South Station with a broad smile and a big hug for me.

As I drove the young people through town, I couldn't help but eavesdrop on their conversations. Someone's brother was back in prison. Another's mother was back on drugs. Nina had a steady job and had finally gotten her own apartment in New York City, only to have various family members suddenly reappear in her life, looking for money or a place to stay. It seemed that every step away from a troubled life brought out the people from that life most in need. She had to set tough limits to avoid being dragged back down.

I pulled up to a dock on the Boston Harbor, where a small ferryboat waited to shuttle us across the water. The youth council was headed to Thompson Island, just a few miles from downtown Boston but a world apart. A perfect location to control the distractions.

The young people dropped their duffle bags in the dormitory and came back to our meeting room, ready to get down to business. I loved the energy and passion these young people brought to the task at hand. They also challenged my stereotypes. The young men usually arrived wearing baggy jeans hanging off their butts, a few with thick gold chains around their necks, the young women with huge gold hoop earrings and long acrylic fingernails. Their physical appearance fed *my* stereotypes of their not-so-distant-past street life.

If I hadn't visited many of their local programs, I might not have recognized how far many of them had come. The majority of students in these programs had grown up in households where nobody got up to go to work. One of the most important skills taught by our programs was not reading or writing but how to get out of bed in the morning. Some programs gave out alarm clocks as part of their orientation. These young people gathered on Thompson Island had traveled a great distance, measured in more ways than miles.

Our youth council members were mostly black and brown, with a few white students from small towns or rural programs. The demographic makeup of the council reflected national statistics of the young people who don't complete high school. These young adults showed up because they had found something here that had been lacking elsewhere in their lives. Each one of them had made the decision to step up and take responsibility. Some still had one leg in the world of their prior lives and would backslide after their involvement with us. Others would go on to become the first in their families to finish high school or attend college. A few years after this gathering, Nina went to law school.

When the proposed program standards were brought to this group, the conversation took a radically different turn from that of their staff counterparts on the directors' council.

"Man, that's giving us *nothing*, if someone can be called a graduate and still don't have a diploma or GED, you know what I mean? Nobody should be called a graduate just because they showed up for ten months. They need to have *earned* it."

It took little debate for them to arrive at a consensus. Most youth council members had been out in the world with nothing but street credentials. They saw this program as their chance to gain a foothold in a previously unattainable world of legal jobs and a stable life. They had too many friends with high school diplomas who were functionally illiterate. They had no question that their peers across the country should be required to complete their GED before they could be called graduates. To them, the false sense of accomplishment of giving out graduation certificates to anyone who had not first attained their GED certificate or diploma was an insult at best.

I began to see how cutting slack to students from tough backgrounds was the worst kind of racism: patronizing and undermining of their abilities. Students like these needed extra support, to be sure. But that was different from lenient standards.

When asked which teachers they liked the best, inevitably these students would identify the ones who were toughest.

"Man, she kicked my butt. But you know, I never would have believed I could be where I am today if it wasn't for that teacher. She didn't give up on me, but she didn't let me off the hook, ever."

By listening to these young people, I learned how school systems throughout the country were full of teachers who took pity on students like them. And they didn't need pity. They needed rigor and discipline.

In fact, a national study done around this time led to similar findings. The Education Trust identified the top performing schools across the country that served high-poverty and high-student-of-color populations. Many of the 4,500 schools studied outperformed predominantly white schools in wealthy communities. These schools educated over two million students across twenty-one states, including about 27 percent African American and 32 percent Latino students. And among the practices they had in common were: extensive use of standards for designing curriculum and instruction, assessing students, and evaluating teachers; significant investment in professional development for teachers to help students meet academic standards; comprehensive systems for monitoring individual student progress and providing extra support when needed; and use of accountability systems with consequences for adults.

In short, these schools set up systems based on the belief that students could perform to high standards. They set up the supports for teachers and students to get there. Then they held the teachers accountable for delivering.

The youth council had settled on program graduation recommendations. Next, they took on attendance standards.

"Yo man, there's no way you can hold down a job out there if you can't learn to show up every day. I know because I tried. Our attendance requirement should be 95 percent, nothing less!"

The adults had wavered on this one, and once again the youth nailed them.

Year after year, I witnessed similar debates. These young people, the cast-offs of public schools from Homestead, Florida, to Bemidji, Minnesota, from East Harlem to East St. Louis, set the toughest standards of all when asked for their opinion.

I had seen what high expectations for struggling students could do back in Boston as well. My TV show had gotten me poking around to find hidden bright spots across the system. Given Boston's dismal dropout rate, I particularly wanted to learn more about Boston's alternative high school programs. These were where the castoffs landed; there were hundreds of teens referred by other schools who couldn't handle them or who left the traditional school programs by choice. Were these programs working? Or just serving as holding tanks?

Community Academy took in the toughest teens. I phoned to arrange a visit. The director was thrilled that a school committee member was willing to take the time to visit her program. On the day of my visit, I pulled up to the warehouse-turned-school-building in the middle of an industrial area adjacent to one of the city's roughest residential neighborhoods. On the inside, young men, mostly African American and dressed in ties and button-down shirts, calmly moved down the hall to their classrooms. This was strikingly different from some of the traditional high schools, where students pushed and shoved and yelled their way through the hallways in between classes.

These were the *bad* kids?

Community Academy was run by a dedicated program director who knew how to practice tough love. She also held her students to high academic standards. She had voluntarily introduced Latin into the curriculum as a required subject. As students greeted her in the hallway, she responded to each by first name.

"Good morning, Daryl. How's that sprained ankle doing?"

"Patrick, has your grandmother found a new apartment yet?"

"Joseph, tuck in your shirt, please. You know the rules here."

I was invited to sit in on a history class, in a small, neat room, metal chairs with small folding desktops arranged in informal clusters. The program director asked for attention.

"Good morning. I'd like you to welcome a special guest we have with us this morning. This is Ms. Naimark, a member of the Boston School Committee."

I was always a bit embarrassed when staff interrupted class for me. I was much more comfortable as an observer. "Thank you for taking the time to have me in your classroom. I'm here because I know our district high schools don't work so well for a lot of students, and I need to better understand the alternatives. I think there might be a lot we can learn from programs like this."

I asked the students what they were learning in history class. One boy raised his hand and described a decidedly Afrocentric curriculum. He ended his description with an apology; they were not really learning what other schools covered.

"But what you are learning is just as important," I responded.

What a sad state of affairs, I thought to myself, *when black teens feel they must apologize for learning about their own history.*

I thanked the students and their teacher and made a quick exit in order to get to work before the morning was over. I was thankful that Boston had at least one effective alternative program.

Boston's high school task force wrapped up its work during the summer I facilitated the youth input to YouthBuild program standards. The task force's plan focused on breaking up all of the underperforming district high schools into smaller learning communities. The teachers union agreed to let go of the forty-two-minute class period, allowing for double blocks of time in key subject areas. Many teachers dragged their feet on this change. *What are we going to do with students for eighty-four minutes?* They could no longer fill the time with rote drills. The task force also pushed to ensure that the district would offer Advanced Placement courses in all high schools.

Within a year, math and English scores started to edge up. Teachers filled the longer class periods with more engaging methods of covering their subjects. Students at the lower performing schools gained access to more challenging courses. Many of the more cynical teachers started to acknowledge that change was possible.

Ultimately, some schools succeeded at creating more nurturing and effective learning communities. Others limped along with the same problems as their predecessors. Like progress on many of the issues we faced, our high schools took two steps forward and one step back.

The next step in Boston's school reform agenda was to update the promotion policy. Over the previous two years, the school committee had approved detailed, grade-by-grade academic standards that I had supported. This was a critical first step toward addressing the uneven quality of curriculum and rigor across our schools.

The proposed new promotion policy was going to end the practice of social promotion, moving students from grade to grade regardless of whether they had met academic requirements. I understood that this practice undermined student achievement. But I was not alone in my reservations about holding students to tough new standards without a corresponding commitment from the adults. Simply expecting more of students with no new requirements of the adults was lopsided. We needed to be sure we were teaching what the students needed to know to be promoted—and teaching it effectively. I also had seen the limitations of relying on standardized tests to know if students understood a subject.

The final promotion policy language was hammered out under pressure to vote immediately on its adoption. It was the last school committee meeting before school let out for the summer, and the superintendent was anxious to have the policy approved. He needed a clear mandate and adequate lead time before the next school year started in September to prepare staff and parents for such a major change in expectations. As committee members haggled over the wording of caveats needed to ensure a passing vote, an animated crowd listened from the audience.

By the time the vote was called, language had been added requiring the school system to implement new support systems for at-risk students and to develop transition programs for students failing to meet the new learning standards. Even with the qualifying language, the new promotion policy barely passed, with three yeas, two nays from Felix and myself, and two members absent from the meeting. Everybody went home hot and tired that night.

At six thirty the next morning, my phone rang. My primary association with calls at this hour was that someone I loved must have died in the night. But I was in for a much better surprise. The unfamiliar male voice on the other end of the line was loud, animated for such an early hour.

"Is this Susan Naimark? I understand you voted against the new promotion policy at last night's school committee meeting. Would you mind talking about it on our radio show?"

No problem. It was a controversial vote, and I had grown accustomed to being the contrarian.

"As a matter of fact, we can put you on the air right now."

I had already completed my sunrise jog around Jamaica Pond, had taken a shower, and was just ironing my clothes when he called. I was ready for him—or so I thought.

"Tell me, Susan, do you really think it's right to pass kids along from grade to grade who can't read and write?"

"No, I just don't think it's right to count on a single test as the only criteria for promotion."

"You mean to tell me you would promote *any* kid even if they don't pass the test?"

"No, that's not what I said."

With each round, the voice on the other end of the line grew louder. Each of his rebounds came quicker than the one before, repeating my statements with just enough changes to turn the meaning into something altogether different. I could tell he was trying to back me into a corner.

"We need to do better at our end as adults before we can hold the students accountable. . . ."

"Oh, I see, you want to let the kids off the hook. . . ."

I again sidestepped his attempt to put words into my mouth. I felt I'd held my own when he finally thanked me and said good-bye. Adrenaline surging, I quickly walked over to my bedside clock radio and tuned in to the show, just in time to hear his final words.

"Boy oh boy, if there were more people like Susan Naimark on school committees across the Commonwealth, we'd be promoting kids based on the color of their eyes."

In fact, the cumulative effects of school tracking, testing, and sorting *did* start with factors as uncontrollable by students as the color of their eyes.

So this was how talk radio worked.

My heart still pounding, I kept the radio on as I got dressed. The first caller began to bring my heart rate down.

"I was one of those kids who never would have graduated from high school if I had to rely on a single, standardized test. I never could pass those tests. I'm a very successful businessman now...."

Vindication.

In the summer of 1998, following passage of Boston's new promotion policy, I once again sought refuge and solutions to Boston's most intractable challenges at the annual conference of the National Coalition of Education Activists. I looked forward to a few days in Washington, DC, where the workshops and camaraderie would help me make sense of the problems I was encountering in Boston.

I heard stories at these conferences that put our work in the Boston Public Schools into perspective. Where I had been outraged by our dropout rate, which in 1998 hovered at 27 or 28 percent, I learned that Cleveland, Memphis, Chicago, and other cities had dropout rates of 50 percent or higher. Our high school class sizes of thirty-five students paled in comparison with New York City, where forty-five students in a class was not unusual.

How could teachers teach and students learn under such conditions?

We talked about race and racism, opportunity and power. At one meeting about parent and community outreach, an older community organizer from Virginia, born in Jamaica, summed up the racism encountered in her work.

"It's like this," she said, covering her red-and-silver Coca-Cola can on the table in front of her with a white paper napkin. "Covered up, all nice and pretty."

The ways in which parents and community members of color were being excluded were no longer blatant or out in the open as in the past. School buses were no longer being stoned, and children of color were no longer prevented by law from attending certain schools. But their education was still lacking, their choices and opportunities still limited. And, as a result, their outcomes were still not like those of the average white child.

Nevertheless, I saw possibilities and bright spots of hope from across the country. I learned about the progressive use of standardized testing in Vermont, put in place before the federal legislation that required all states to use such tests for passing or failing students. Vermont had figured out how to use them in a more nuanced way. These tests were only given to a sampling of students to assess each school's overall progress. This approach minimized the amount of time taken away from teaching for testing. It also eliminated the use of these tests as a single make-or-break way of knowing if students understood their subjects.

I learned about action research projects in New York City that got students out in the community, gathering data on community concerns and developing strategies to address them. I heard about schools in Portland, Oregon, that had eliminated ability-based tracking and showed impressive academic results for all students.

I was inspired and wanted more. That summer, I threw my name in for the organization's steering committee and was elected at the conference. I needed another commitment like a hole in my head. But I was on a roll.

I loved being the one nobody could keep up with; I was buoyed when my friends said, "I don't know how you do it—you're amazing." Besides, I was beginning to make a difference. I was reaching the dreams I had had since I was a teenager but could never say aloud because who was I to think I could move mountains, or even foothills? Just a quiet kid with grand ideas rolling around in her head about wanting to make a difference in the world.

I'm not even sure where these dreams came from. But my father had been instrumental in building alliances between the Jewish and black communities in Detroit. And my mother always said to us kids, "You are so lucky. You can be whatever you want to be." She also regularly reminded us that Jewish people in Germany before the rise of Hitler were as integrated and accepted in the larger society as any time or place in our people's history. In other words, don't ever get too comfortable.

And to be sure we didn't get too comfortable, the religious school I attended three times each week throughout my childhood showed film footage of the Nazi concentration camps to every class, every year. These films started when we were very young; we saw terrifying images of skeletal people, barely alive, with big hollow eyes; piles and piles of bones; the tall chimneys of the gas chambers. My parents' generation, who came of age during World War II, wanted to be sure we would never forget the horrors that were possible in our seemingly civilized world. As a young child, I tried not to look at those scary images on the screen in the front of the classroom. But the message sank in loud and clear: wherever there is injustice, we Jews could always be its next target.

My drive to make a difference was well embedded by the time I went up against the Boston Public Schools. The more injustice I saw and experienced, the more I needed to do something about it.

At the same time, I was not getting enough peace and quiet, time for reflection, time for family, time for myself, time to breathe. I was becoming the person I always wanted to be, but in the process I felt more distant from people I cared about. I had been running on empty for so many years now that I didn't know how to stop. This was no way to have a life. By the summer of 1998, I knew that something had to give.

With John's encouragement, I signed up for Outward Bound. I would spend ten days at sea off the coast of Maine before school swung into gear in September. I didn't know anything about sailing, but I loved the ocean, and I needed to get away from everything. It would be ten days during which my only worries would be the wind, the waves, and keeping my clothes dry.

The sailing was fun, but what really captured my imagination was our day on the ropes course, something new and totally outside my comfort zone. The "Elvis" high-wire walk was a thick wire cable suspended between two platforms twenty feet above the ground, with another parallel cable stretched another fifteen feet above the first. I climbed the ladder to the platform at one end of the high wire. We were instructed to walk along the wire like a tightrope, holding on to a rope dangling from the overhead cable. As soon as you walked a few steps, you had to let go of the dangling rope and grab for the next one. The first two ropes were close enough together so that you could grab the second one without letting go of the first. But then the rest of the dangling ropes were spaced farther apart so that you had to let go of one before you could reach for the next, which meant that the only way to walk the entire length of cable was to lunge from dangling rope to dangling rope.

I stepped off the platform. In that instant of lunging forward, my feet planted on the high wire, my upper body was momentarily suspended between ropes. Twenty feet above the ground, I leaned forward, hanging on to nothing. As I made my way along the tightrope, I slipped several times trying to grab the dangling ropes. Each fall left me hanging by my safety suspenders, unharmed. Even knowing this, I couldn't get myself to let go of the rope. It required a true leap of faith. My mind said, *Go,* but my arms refused to budge. I eventually made it across—I have no idea how.

This Outward Bound trip was full of metaphors.

Deciding to go for the seat on the Boston School Committee, and agreeing to take it when offered, had been a huge leap into the unknown. It hadn't been driven by faith so much as determination, although a strong sense of faith in what's possible was certainly required.

On school committee, I had become frustrated that I wasn't taking more risks. I had no problem voting my conscience, but I didn't go the next step often enough and convince others to support alternative scenarios. In Outward Bound, all the activities required a careful assignment of people to keep an eye on the ones taking the plunge. Outward Bound made me recognize the relationship between taking risks and lining up people to watch my back.

Still intimidated by the powerful people I found myself surrounded by, I fled out the door after school committee meetings. Sure, I was tired and wanted to get home. We all did. Yet, despite my appearance of bravado, I was scared.

Of what?

Showing my vulnerabilities.

Doing something stupid.

Making contact.

For all my activity, I too often felt isolated and unsure of myself.

Sometimes I felt like Walter Mitty, the fictitious character who alternates precariously between his quiet, unobtrusive self and delusions of power and grandeur. Which was the real me? I wasn't sure.

After Outward Bound, I began to escape almost every Saturday morning for a long run on Nantasket Beach, twenty miles south of Boston. My weekend runs, with the crashing waves at my side, restored my equilibrium, if briefly. If the weather was good, I set up my beach chair and brought along my never-ending school committee reading. My soul slowly came back into alignment as the sea lapped gently along the beach. My weekly half-day of downtime held tremendous possibilities.

On those weekends where I felt pressed for time, John encouraged me. He, too, was hopeful that my weekly beach trips would bring me back to life—and to him.

I sometimes thought about the parents I knew who didn't have the resources for anything like Outward Bound, or the luxury of driving to the beach every Saturday morning. If they took time off at all, it was for a road trip to visit family or to take care of an ailing parent. I thought about those who get involved in organizing campaigns to improve their children's schools: How did they keep going? My respect for parents in such circumstances grew when I compared their lives to my own.

That fall, the Boston School Committee was faced with finding ways to ensure that students could meet our new promotion standards. After my contrary vote on the new promotion policy two months earlier, Liz, who was now the school committee chair, did what any astute leader would do. She appointed me to head up the new Promotion Policy Task Force to figure out how to implement the policy I had just voted against.

As head of the task force, I was charged to work with one of the deputy superintendents to assemble a team and develop recommendations for implementing the new policy. Liz and I emailed back and forth with names of people we each wanted on the task force. I recommended active parents and community advocates who I thought were closest to the ground and most understanding of the student perspective. The school committee chair wanted to ensure we had a broad base that covered various constituencies, such as cultural and technology organizations, and educational experts with benchmarking experience.

We finally agreed on a list. It included Ms. Leonard, my sons' principal at the Trotter, who was now a widely respected middle school principal; a representative from the local teachers union; parent organization representatives; after-school program providers; educational advocates; and two high school students. My excitement mounted about the possibilities for solving a central piece of the school reform puzzle. I placed phone calls to prospective task force members, who one by one responded that they were honored to serve.

We called our first meeting as the new school year opened that fall, holding it in the superintendent's conference room at school department headquarters. As task force members introduced themselves around the polished wood conference table, I delighted at being at the center of such an important task. Maybe we really could figure out how to create the right balance of high standards and quality supports needed to ensure all students had a fighting chance of success.

As the new task force took up the charge to instill more rigor and support across the system, Boston Latin School beat my son Ben over the head with its unique brand of rigor.

The task force began to meet in September 1998, when Ben entered his senior year of high school. He frequently stayed up until midnight to finish his homework and worried about his grade point average and whether he was taking enough Advanced Placement courses. John and I had to remind him that his sleep was more important than getting an A on every homework assignment.

Ben's senior year featured a prominent posting of each student's class rank on the bulletin board outside of the guidance counselors' office. Students and parents began to receive weekly admonitions about the college application process, with notes sent home about "safety" schools and "stretch" schools.

"Be sure to apply to at least a few of both."

"Don't forget to schedule your college visits."

"Your English teacher should be reviewing draft personal statements by now."

"See your guidance counselor for financial aid forms."

My head spun through most of the process. My own college entry had followed a single application to the state public university. I tried to take it all in, alternating between annoyance and intimidation. Ben had bought into Boston Latin's drive and wanted badly to get into a "name-brand" college. I pushed back when he asked for John and me to pay for an SAT prep course.

"But, Ben, you did fine on the SAT! We're going to be spending enough money on college, and you have the grades and scores to get into a great school. I don't see why we need to spend money on making you more competitive!"

"But, Mom, all the other kids are doing it. You don't understand! If I could just break 1400—that's what a lot of the schools are looking for. You're putting me at a *disadvantage* by not letting me take the prep course."

I thought about the students in most of Boston's other high schools, who were unlikely to have a guidance counselor to talk to at all. It was rare for students in the district high schools to receive any guidance about the college application process. Advantage was a relative concept.

We didn't pay for the prep course, and Ben found extra help at school that partially compensated. He applied early admission and was accepted to the University of Chicago, a highly competitive, high-priced university.

While Ben worked on the umpteenth draft of his college application essay, the Promotion Policy Task Force spent the fall months studying reams of academic performance data assembled by school department research staff. We debated strategies and priorities. We divided into work groups that delved into the details of three key areas that needed attention: communication, student support, and measuring progress.

What would it really take to get all students up to speed, giving them a fighting chance of meeting the new standards?

By December, the promotion policy work groups had each presented their findings to the full task force, and these were synthesized into a report to school committee. The complexity of the challenge did not lend itself to simple solutions. Detailed recommendations addressed the need for better communication with students and parents to be sure they understood the new policies and support services available, expanded partnerships with community organizations to provide the necessary supports, well-defined benchmarks, and an ongoing monitoring group to assess progress.

As a result of these recommendations, when the next budget vote came around in the spring, the school committee moved $21 million into extra supports for students at risk of failing. I was making a difference, and the adrenaline rush kept me going.

Boston was slowly closing the achievement gap, at the same time as we were reducing dropout rates. Too many other cities were pushing low-performing students out of school as their way of bringing up aggregate test scores. Boston began to offer advanced coursework in our nonexam high schools. We still weren't talking much about race, but we were addressing some of the underlying problems that made up modern-day racism. And it was making a difference.

Yet the racial achievement gap persisted. We still needed to talk about race. One hot summer evening, Superintendent Payzant brought to our school committee meeting the latest report on students' standardized test scores. As we sat in our designated seats on the platform that was our monthly Wednesday evening home, my colleague Felix leaned into his microphone to express his concern over the failing scores of black and Latino students. They were still close to double the failure rates of the white and Asian students.

In response, I noted some examples of school districts, including Toronto and Milwaukee, that had adopted explicit anti-racist policies and a commitment to training school staff in strategies that actively worked to dismantle racist patterns of behavior. It seemed simple enough to me. If students of color were disproportionately failing, it behooved all of us to better understand the racial dynamics at play. This exchange between Felix and me was met with polite nods from our colleagues. As usual, there were no comments.

When the meeting ended, a white high school teacher marched up to me, red-faced. "I'm sorry, Ms. Naimark, but I have a real problem with what you just said up there. Just because students are failing the tests does not mean we're all racists. I'm so tired of being looked at like that. You don't know how hard I work with my kids, and so do most teachers I know. I find your remarks incredibly insensitive…."

I heard her out and tried my best to keep my voice measured as I responded. These were always the most challenging conversations, for which I had to steel myself. How to explain in a few sentences what had taken me years to understand, while anticipating the defensiveness that was so often the first reaction of white people to any discussion about racism?

"I think there are things we all do that may not be consciously racist but that undermine children of color. I was not up there saying that all teachers are racist, just that we need to better understand how our own behavior affects children. . . ."

In fact, I had come to believe that all white people *are* racist. We are racist in the sense that we hold on to the benefits that come to us effortlessly, and we don't believe it is our responsibility to intervene when "the way things have always been" puts people of color at a distinct disadvantage. This kind of racism may be unconscious, but it is not benign. But I knew the reaction that analysis was likely to elicit, so I kept it to myself.

The teacher softened a bit once she had gotten the rage off her chest and realized I was willing to hear her out. I tried to frame my thoughts to find a common starting point between us.

"We have to both agree that it's the black and Latino students who are disproportionately failing in our schools, right? Well, there are lots of things influencing this that are bigger than either of us. I just think we need to make an effort to better understand them."

"Okay, I see your point. But that's not the same as saying we're racist."

I thought she heard me this time around, and I didn't want to lose momentum. "What happens in our schools isn't isolated. Whatever is happening to those kids out in the community, they're bringing that into school with them. I'm not saying our schools are more racist than other places, just that they are part of the whole picture that is not working for these kids."

This teacher's reaction should not have surprised me. But until we learn to have open and honest conversations about the things, big and small, that white people do, whether knowingly or otherwise, that smack of racism to people of color, we limit our ability to support children of color in our schools. The things we do like being quicker to single out black boys than white boys as troublemakers, or dominating a meeting and not realizing that we might be intimidating someone with valuable experience and perspective on the topic at hand. Some of the changes I was hoping this teacher would consider had less to do with policies and standards and everything to do with the attitudes and the atmosphere within our schools.

John had come up against the unbending atmosphere in the schools for years, trying to offer himself as a volunteer. After a number of false starts, he had begun to volunteer on a regular basis back at the Trotter School. And he loved it. He began to raise the idea of becoming an elementary school teacher. The summer after Ben's high school graduation, he made the leap. He went back to school for his teaching credential and was assigned his first classroom at the Paul A. Dever Elementary School in Boston.

As John set up his classroom that August, the veteran teachers filtered into the building to prepare for a new school year. An older white teacher across the hall welcomed him.

"Good luck. You're going to have twenty-two animals and one or two kids you can really teach."

In our house, she became known as the Twenty-Two Animals Teacher. I never knew her name. The scariest part was realizing that one-third of the students in the school would have this teacher for fourth grade. In fourth grade children become keenly aware of their self-identity and begin to form their views of where they fit into the world. The potential damage of that one teacher to a full third of the students in that school was frightening.

I wanted to believe that the Twenty-Two Animals Teacher was an isolated example. But experience had taught me otherwise. Such teachers may be a minority, but it only took a few of them to poison the learning environment. This problem of attitudes and expectations went beyond technical fixes.

During my tenure on the Boston School Committee, I spent five years in a daytime job listening to our country's most disenfranchised youth as I traveled the country working with alternative education programs for low-income high school dropouts. I learned that these young people were frequently the smartest children growing up. They took stock of their options in too-often dysfunctional schools and communities and families, and they made the decision that their schools were not going to give them what they needed to thrive—or even survive. They were often the ones who chafed most at authority; they were creative and independent-spirited. Aren't creativity and independence core American values?

When I sat with these young people, one-on-one or in group settings, they were consistently engaged, caring, and resourceful. They understood the problems in the schools as well as anyone and frequently came up with solutions within their alternative education programs that made the programs work. I began to speculate: What if we extended this model to our public schools? Why do we have to wait until young people are ejected from public schools and then ask for their input to reconstruct success in alternative programs?

A radical proposition began to take shape in my mind as I traveled the country and returned to face off with Boston's failing high schools.

What if, for an entire school year, we shut down every high school that wasn't getting acceptable results for a significant percentage of its students? And we then brought together the students, staff, families, and community organizations to reinvent the school? That year, the students would get full credit for hands-on, real-time learning.

The students would learn math by studying taxation, state revenue streams, and school budgetary needs. They would learn history and social studies by studying federal, state, and local educational laws and policies, labor unions, community demographics, and voting patterns. They would learn reading and writing by developing recommendations and presenting them to the larger community.

School staff would facilitate this process, using their skills as teachers and guides to support students to learn the relevant information.

Community organizations would reach out to parents and grandparents, local businesses, and other neighborhood residents. They would organize community forums, encourage participation, and serve as bridges between the larger community and each school.

Everybody would debate and discuss and negotiate until they agreed on a way to proceed. Maybe all the schools in a city would come together from time to time throughout this special school year, building relationships and shared agreements. By the time the schools reopened the following September, everybody would know their role and responsibilities. And the community would have a shared vision for its schools.

Is this such a radical idea?

CHAPTER EIGHT

On Metal Detectors & Other Priorities

FOR SEVERAL YEARS RUNNING, I accepted neatly handwritten invitations from the Patrick Gavin Middle School Politics Club to come to their classroom and talk about school committee.

In February 1999 I decided to focus my lesson on the school system budget. The school committee had recently approved higher promotion and graduation standards. We were in the midst of debate about how to provide extra supports to ensure that students across Boston could meet those new standards. The Gavin Politics Club offered perfect timing to seek the advice of a classroom of thirteen-year-olds.

I arrived to an expectant classroom of eighth graders looking forward to their forty-two-minute break from the usual routine. My plan was to put the students in my seat for the class period, starting with a carefully prepared explanation of my role in terms a thirteen-year-old could understand.

"The school committee is like the boss of your principal. We hire the superintendent, and he hires your school principal. We also set rules for the schools and decide how to spend the money for all the schools. This year, we have to figure out how to be sure that all kids can be promoted because there are new graduation rules that are harder than the old ones.

"We have $5 million to spend this year to help students who are failing."

I wrote the figure on the blackboard in front of the class to emphasize the magnitude of the task at hand. I had decided in advance to keep the numbers simple. The actual school department budget was approaching the half-billion-dollar mark. I didn't want to overwhelm the students.

"Here are the choices we're considering: We can pay for special tutors for the students who are failing; we can pay for teacher training; we can pay for smaller kindergarten classes; or we can pay for special after-school programs for middle school students to help them get ready for high school."

I listed the very real proposals on the blackboard, under the $5 million figure.

"We know that too many kids who are failing don't even get noticed until it's too late. Special tutors would give them extra attention in elementary school, as soon as they start to fall behind. We also realize that some teachers are more effective than others with their students. Extra teacher training could help them get better at teaching. Kindergarten is a long way off from high school, but a lot of people think that the kids who are behind in high school often start out behind from the very beginning. Maybe they weren't read to at home or aren't good at sitting and following instructions in kindergarten. Smaller kindergarten classes would help some of these kids get a better start. The last proposal comes from what a lot of high school teachers say, that kids come into high school behind. We need to catch them up before they start high school."

I then asked for five volunteers to serve as the school committee. I en couraged the rest to sign up for public comment to weigh in before the vote. The "school committee" members were instructed to listen to their peers and then decide how to spend the money. They came up to the front of the classroom, sat down in the five chairs I had pulled up in front of the teacher's desk, and called on their classmates for input.

After much deliberation, the Gavin School Politics Club rejected all the proposals on the table. They decided instead to use the money to buy metal detectors for the high schools.

Where did this *come from?*

Their decision didn't reflect any of the options I had so carefully laid out. Once again, the young people put me in my place, reminding me that we adults did not have all the answers. Or maybe even the right questions.

The students then explained their decision. "Well, the big kids can tutor the little kids, so you don't need to pay money for that. The teachers already went to school to become teachers, so they don't need more training.

And kindergartners don't have to pass tests, so we don't need to spend money to make their classes smaller...."

And then I realized that here was a group of thirteen-year-olds who were scared to death of what they expected to face when they went off to high school next year. They had undoubtedly heard stories from older siblings or bigger kids in their neighborhoods about scuffles in the hallways and more serious offenses in the street after school let out. They were keenly aware of the imminent transition from being the oldest among preadolescents to becoming the youngest among full-blown teenagers. The potential threat to their own safety eclipsed any impending academic challenges that might have been on their minds.

I didn't bring the recommendations of the Gavin Politics Club back to school committee. But I think about this session often. It is a reminder that we cannot separate students' needs into neat little buckets, only address the ones that are labeled "academic," and then expect them to succeed. When students come to school feeling unsafe, the resources poured into curriculum development will not make them feel safer unless we find creative ways to connect curriculum to the challenges of their real lives. At the same time, we also have to find ways to connect with outside resources that address crime and safety issues.

This is so much bigger than most school districts think. Schools by themselves cannot solve all of the community problems that surround them. But they can do a much better job of building bridges with others who are working to solve those problems. I was to spend many months mulling over what that could look like.

In 1999, the Boston Public Schools' real half-billion-dollar budget translated to an average of $8,500 spent on each of 64,000 students.

Every year at budget time people asked, usually in deep frustration, "But where does all that money *go?*"

Three-quarters of the budget went toward salaries and benefits. Education is a labor-intensive effort, with over four thousand teachers on payroll in Boston that year. While Boston Public School teachers had higher salaries than their counterparts in most other big cities, they also had to contend with one of the highest costs of living in the country. I always laid low during union contract negotiations when it was the school committee's job as management to hold the line on salaries. Hard-working and effective teachers earn every dollar and deserve to be paid whatever we can afford for doing such an important job in our society. My particular belief on this issue did not correspond to the interests or official position of management.

Boston spending increased from $8,500 to $9,000 per student within the next few years as we invested in smaller class sizes, new instructional materials, expanded professional development for teachers, and three new early education centers—all of the strategies rejected by my young advisors from the Gavin School.

This level of spending allowed for class sizes that ranged from twenty-two students in grades kindergarten through second to thirty-one in high school. These class sizes, while smaller than many other urban school districts, were still way above suburban and private schools. They were an improvement, but hardly ideal for allowing teachers to give students the attention they needed to succeed.

The budget also provided a basic set of textbooks that were updated on a five-year cycle, and $58 per student for other instructional supplies, including replacement books during the years between the new purchases. Many teachers spent hundreds of dollars out of their own pockets every year to set up their classrooms. The core budget did not cover such "frills." The other big-ticket items in the budget included special needs services, facilities maintenance, and utility bills.

We kept up with the bills during my tenure on the school committee, thanks in large part to a supportive mayor who ensured that the school department budget received incremental boosts within the city budget from year to year. But there were never enough funds to cover the most basic needs. High schools were allotted one guidance counselor for every three hundred students. Elementary schools with enrollments of three hundred or fewer were managed by a principal supported by a single secretary.

It always angered me when people asked how we could spend "so much." Boston and the New England region have a long tradition of private schools, many of which have highly competitive application processes, where people don't hesitate to pay three times as much as we were spending per student. Public schools have an open-door policy that precludes the type of selectivity that ensures success at so many private schools. And yet we were asked why we couldn't succeed at one-third of the price tag of the private schools.

As school committee struggled with reallocating resources to get our district high schools up to par, Ben's Boston Latin graduation arrived in June 1999. The graduation ceremony was preceded by an invitation to the school's annual Prize Night. With over 350 years' worth of graduates, the school's alumni association had built up an endowment that now funded $1 million in scholarships distributed to graduating seniors each year. With too many scholarships to hand out at the graduation ceremony, the venue for Prize Night was a downtown auditorium that could seat over a thousand people.

Virtually every graduate received something, from a few hundred dollars left behind by a class from the 1890s to reward public spirit, to several full four-year scholarships offered to all of Boston's high schools by Boston University.

As happy as I was for Ben, my mind kept wandering to Boston's nonexam high schools. Boston Latin had the highest percentage of white, middle-class students of any public school in Boston. The district high schools that most needed this type of scholarship support had little to offer their own students. I always wondered why nobody sued the Boston School Committee over the glaring inequities.

I also thought back to Ben's insistence on the need for SAT tutoring. Private tutoring was now turning into big business across the country. The year Ben graduated, Princeton Review started offering private tutorial programs for the SAT. Sylvan Learning Centers saw growth in its tutoring services for high achieving students. More families who could afford it were paying thousands of dollars for these services to give their children an additional competitive edge.

We are all familiar with the American saying that education is the great equalizer. But how can we get to equality of opportunity if we must rely on individual resources to ensure our children's academic success? It was becoming clearer to me all the time that public funding of education needed to drastically expand and that "the basics" needed to include whatever it takes to ensure all children have access to the supports necessary for success. I think across the ocean to Finland, where the goal of public education is equity, and quality has followed in equity's footsteps. This shift requires political will and a national acceptance of all children as *our* children.

I began reading about the civil rights movement, wanting to better understand how social change happens, how movements are born and grow. One account particularly stuck in my mind: the story of a student who had dropped out of college in the North and gone south to help. He described how volunteers showed up in large numbers, from everywhere, and were put right to work, assigned something useful to do. People were getting killed, and there was a deep sense of urgency.

Weren't children getting killed—if not physically, certainly academically and spiritually—now? I had neighbors who tried calling our local high school to offer to help out, and their phone calls were never returned. It took John five years to get in the door as a volunteer in our sons' elementary school.

Where was our collective sense of urgency?

The Boston school system's centuries-old tradition of inviting the highest-performing students to exam schools perennially left the rest of the city's students behind. And as long as those in power could get their students into these selective schools, there would be no sense of urgency among the people who called the shots. When my sons got to Boston Latin School, I discovered that the children of a majority of the city's leaders went there. This shouldn't have surprised me. I often wondered how many of these public officials and corporate leaders had ever set foot in one of the city's district high schools. Boston's district high schools operated in a world far from Boston Latin School.

I attended the Jeremiah E. Burke High School graduation ceremony in 2001. It was the first year in the school's history that every graduate had applied to and been accepted into college.

The Burke, as it is known, sits in Grove Hall, the heart of Boston's African American community. Generations of black families proudly associated with the school through its ups and downs over many decades. In 1995, the Burke and several other Boston high schools lost their accreditation. Many schools across the country, including all of New York

City's public high schools, function without the external stamp of approval of regional accreditation boards. Boston's high schools, all previously accredited, lost their standing that year as a result of inadequate facilities, poor-quality instruction, and too low a ratio of guidance counselors to students. A political embarrassment at best, it sent a chill through the system. Students graduating from these schools worried whether this downgrade in status would affect their ability to get into college. It added yet one more disadvantage to their prospects.

Dr. Leonard, a seasoned headmaster with roots in the local community, had been brought in to turn the Burke around when it lost accreditation. A tall, stocky, African American man with a charming smile, he had a doctorate in education and a forceful management style. He had worked in the Boston Public Schools long enough to know his way around, and he wasn't shy about advocating for what he needed to resuscitate the beleaguered school. He was also the husband of our sons' elementary school principal back at the Trotter.

The Burke was a fighting school, if nothing else. When it lost accreditation, the parents mobilized. Michele, a Burke parent and herself a graduate of the school, was working part-time at the school at the time. Starting as a volunteer when her daughter entered the school, she had quit her job as a quality assurance test engineer to run the Burke Family Center. A tall African American woman with a partiality for large brass earrings and bracelets, Michele was fierce in her loyalties. When Dr. Leonard was brought in to get the school back on its feet, he secured funding to hire Michele, and charged her to increase parent involvement in the school.

The school had first received notice from the regional accreditation board that it was being placed on "warning" status in 1992. The warning cited, among other items, outdated facilities and too few guidance counselors. The parents arranged meetings with the superintendent and school committee. The chair of the school committee at the time, an African American man who sympathized with their plight, explained how the budget worked and told them to go after whatever resources they needed to correct the situation. Reassured about the school committee's ability to address the problem, the parents invited its chair, their new ally, to speak when the Burke Family Center opened. With his encouragement, Burke parents were optimistic that funding would be secured to address the problems and satisfy the accreditation board.

Two years later, they received a letter from the accreditation board stating that the school had been further downgraded from warning to probation. The parents attempted to reach out to the other high schools in the same situation but were unable to get past unresponsive headmasters. They asked for support from the citywide parent council and got no response. Mayor Menino, then serving as acting mayor, assured the Burke parents that he would not let the school lose accreditation. The next year, 1995, the Burke received notice that it had lost accreditation.

Michele's voice rose when she described what happened next.

"When we got the notice that the school was losing accreditation, the parents went ballistic. We organized some teams to strategize. Our first option was to reach out to parents from prior years and file a class action suit. We had been lied to. We were mad. Everybody had insisted it wasn't going to happen. We contacted the lawyer from the earlier [Boston Public Schools] desegregation case. He took us on and laid out our options. He said the class action suit would take years. He recommended going to the federal Office of Civil Rights. We would have to be able to make the case of discrimination.

"Boston Tech had just been renovated to move Boston Latin Academy there. Two parents went and asked for a tour. They wrote down all the things they saw that were new. They compared demographics, since these were two schools in the same neighborhood. We took pictures in our school. We looked at teacher-student ratios. We had a large special education population, almost 30 percent. We realized that about 60 percent of our kids lived within a two-mile radius of the school, so we looked at neighborhood demographics. We said, 'This is the darkest, poorest school. Our kids come from families that have eleventh grade average educational attainment. We have endured these cuts and these are the results.'

"The girls' bathrooms had no stalls. We had a championship basketball team that played in a gym with humps in the floor. If it rained, you couldn't see in the gym, the lights were so dim. We had the same science labs that were there when I was a student. I knew because a burn mark I had made as a student was still there."

From this information, their attorney created thirty-five points that needed to be addressed, and the parents filed an official complaint with the federal Office of Civil Rights. With the complaint came notice to the school district that all federal funds would be withheld if they didn't reach agreement with the Burke parents within ninety days on a plan to rectify the identified problems.

The initial response of the school department was a plan for $800,000 in improvements. The parents established a negotiating team, and by the end of negotiations, the commitment increased to over $5 million. Rewiring the school required a new electrical transformer in the neighborhood. The school was painted, new science labs installed, and the library expanded. The plan also specified smaller class sizes, enough adults to work closely with all students, and the addition of Advanced Placement courses.

The school regained its accreditation in 1998.

A short three years later, getting every graduate accepted into college was no small feat. Other district high schools in Boston hovered between 55 percent and 65 percent college-going rates for their graduates. When I asked Dr. Leonard how he did it, he responded with a grin.

"I told the seniors they *couldn't* graduate if they didn't apply to college."

He had been a high school football player and had served in the marines in Vietnam. Students and staff alike didn't challenge his word lightly. This simple statement said much about how expectations affect student outcomes.

Yet Dr. Leonard worried that the staffing and budget he had been allocated as a result of the civil rights case would last only as long as it took to regain accreditation.

"There is nothing extra at the Burke," he told me one day. "In reality, what it takes to run the Burke effectively is pretty close to what it really takes to run any Boston high school effectively."

Once the Burke was back on track, the court order was lifted and the budget brought back in line with other Boston high schools—that is to say, lowered. By 2003, the school had lost thirty-seven staff positions, class size went back up, and academic achievement went back down. Dr. Leonard had moved on by then.

All was not lost, however. Subsequently, the Burke received additional funding for extensive new facilities, including a new gym and library to be built adjacent to the original 1920s school building. Michele's assessment was this: "The Burke is getting a new building because Project Right [a local community organization] never let go of the original promise."

A community-based organizing group provided the continuity to hold the Boston School Department to its commitments. Project Right's paid organizers worked with resident volunteers who never lost sight of the need for a high-quality high school in their community. Between staff and volunteers, they stayed on top of annual city and school department budgets year after year, advocating for the resources needed to fulfill their dream.

Other district high schools did not have advocates like this. If they did, maybe they could have thrown their collective weight behind a citywide strategy. Maybe the political will that I saw sorely lacking could have been built. Maybe more low-income students and students of color across the city could get the educational resources they deserved.

I could see that grassroots organizing was a missing piece of the answer to our schools' challenges. Given that those in power had better options for their own children's education, the only way to build power among those without those options was to organize. Their collective power would be able to sway the city to allocate the resources that otherwise went elsewhere.

More recent research has documented the impact of grassroots organizing on school reform. Organized groups in urban and rural communities across the country have built the power to change resource allocation as well as ineffective and harmful school policies and practices. And once low-income communities are organized, they can hold the system accountable, as Project Right did in Boston.

I always knew the children in Boston deserved more than the school system provided. Then an economic downturn swept across the country and hit school departments and municipal budgets everywhere. In March 2002, the Boston School Committee faced the untenable choice of laying off 20 percent of the teachers or approving a budget without adequate projected revenue to back it up.

As I contemplated our options, I remembered back to the last economic recession a decade earlier, when I was so infuriated at disruptive midyear teacher layoffs at my sons' elementary school. At the time, I couldn't understand how school committee could have approved a budget without knowing where the money would come from to cover it. New taxes were not on the table this time around, as a statewide referendum the previous year had resoundingly defeated that option.

In my own childhood, I learned early on that you don't spend what you don't have. But forgoing music lessons or family vacations to be sure the basics were covered was, in the end, a personal choice my parents made. Laying off almost a thousand teachers was another matter.

I had no idea how to vote. It wouldn't be responsible to pass a budget knowing the funds weren't there to cover it. And it wouldn't be *right* to pass a budget that further cut resources to an already underfunded system.

The week before the budget vote, I flew to Detroit to be with my father for an unexpected surgery. It was fairly routine, and he didn't make a big deal about it, except to say that he needed someone to drive him to the hospital and home the next day. When the doctor informed us, after the operation, that he shouldn't drive for another few days, I selfishly registered relief. This was the excuse I needed for not returning to Boston for the budget vote.

This was not a resolution of which I was proud. In other difficult committee votes, I consumed a tremendous amount of moral and mental energy sorting out my position and seeking creative alternatives to any proposal I opposed. This year's budget vote remained one of the few times during my school committee tenure when I could not come to terms with a decision we were charged to make. The outcome would be the same whether I was present for the vote or not. Despite having found an acceptable cover for my absence, my lack of a position on that budget vote haunted me.

I stayed in Detroit, and the drastically reduced budget passed school committee vote with no opposition and one member absent. The ensuing teacher layoffs rocked the system. Virtually all of the newer teachers who hadn't yet secured tenure were let go. Seniority then dictated which teachers would fill remaining positions, causing massive shuffling and bumping from one school to another. Class sizes were maxed out, support staff became even scarcer, and holes emerged in previous pockets of success.

A few months later, still unsettled by the recently downgraded school department budget, I found myself in Canton, Ohio, for my job. In my hotel room after delivering an afternoon workshop, I turned on the television just in time for the local newscast.

"We've got good news for our viewers: taxes are going down next year!"

My thoughts veered to the school committee vote that resulted in the reduction of Boston's teaching force by eight hundred teachers, a full 20 percent of the teaching staff. By now, cities and towns across the country were instituting fees for high school sports participation and trash collection. And I thought, what if that newscaster had said, "Great news for residents: all community sports programs and trash collection will be eliminated next year!"

The spin this newscaster put on taxes was disheartening at best and disingenuous at worst. And it continues to this day.

The "no new taxes" drumbeat overlooks what our taxes pay for. We somehow take for granted schools, roads, police and fire protection, even unemployment checks when a family member gets laid off. Too many politicians and opinion makers have led the public to disconnect these basic services from the funding that pays for them. The naysayers paint a picture of poor people and communities of color somehow sucking these resources undeservedly away from the rest of us—the rest of us being white, middle- and upper-class people, who expect these same basic services for ourselves.

Public education is considered a state's responsibility in the United States, but the inequities are a national problem. As states and local municipalities tighten their fiscal belts, the federal government must step up.

One year before the 2002 round of Boston budget cuts, school accountability systems began taking hold across the country. President Bush approved a federal budget that included $42 billion for schools and $300 billion for military expenditures. His education budget looked like a significant increase over the prior year, in recognition of the new requirements of the No Child Left Behind Act of 2001 (NCLB). Yet it barely covered the extra testing requirements, never mind support for an enriched curriculum, smaller class sizes, more competitive teacher salaries, or the myriad other improvements that have shown positive results.

NCLB's stated goals are to improve the performance of schools and the academic achievement of students, specifically including those who are economically disadvantaged. Following the law's passage, the U.S. General Accounting Office (now called the Government Accountability Office) was asked to study differences in school spending and how they might affect our nation's ability to meet this goal. Here is what it found:

> Factors that may relate to student achievement differed between inner city and suburban schools in our study. Research has shown a positive relationship between student achievement and factors such as teacher experience, lower enrollment, more library books and computer resources, and higher levels of parental involvement. Among the 24 schools we visited, the average student achievement scores were generally lower in inner city than in suburban schools. Along with lower achievement scores, these inner city schools were more likely to have a higher percentage of first-year teachers, whose lack of experience can be an indicator of lower teacher quality. In addition, in comparison to the suburban schools, inner city schools generally were older, had higher student enrollments, and had fewer library books per pupil and less technological support.

After passing the federal law that required school districts across the country to raise achievement, the same federal government identified a significant lack of resources to meet the new requirements. This has been a set up for failure from the beginning.

Even before the passage of NCLB, our federal government's preference for military spending over education spending was out of control. In 1998, Congress passed and President Clinton signed a federal budget that included $1 billion the Pentagon didn't want. These funds were for continued development of weapons to defend the United States against missile attacks, weapons that had already received over $45 billion in investment and had yet to be successfully produced. The director of the Pentagon's ballistic missile defense office said at the time, "There really is nothing we can do with additional money that we haven't already addressed."

The military weapons lobby had trumped even the Pentagon. Since then, U.S. military spending has continued at ten times the level of federal education spending. A billion dollars could buy a lot of library books and guidance counselors.

Research has also shown a correlation between high school dropouts and burgeoning prison budgets. Since 2003, the United States has had the highest incarceration rate of any nation on earth. More recent research by Northeastern University's Center for Labor Market Studies found that male high school dropouts of all races were forty-seven times more likely to be incarcerated than their peers who had graduated from college. Black male high school dropouts had the highest rates of incarceration, at 23 percent. The cost of this trajectory is over $292,000 for each dropout over the course of their lifetime, in lost wages, incarceration, health care, and other services. Taxpayers who foot this bill would pay less if they supported investment in quality public education at the front end.

In 1980, the U.S. government spent $27 billion on education and $8 billion on corrections. Fifteen years later, in 1995, federal appropriations for corrections surpassed funding for elementary and secondary education for the first time. Since then, state budgets from Rhode Island to California have been steadily sinking under the weight of ever-swelling prison spending, while education spending continues to atrophy. Even the most tough-on-crime advocates are beginning to see that this is not a rational trade-off.

Our country's shortcomings in educational investment have not been because state and federal governments don't have money. They are the result of how we allocate the resources we have. As long as we see the nation's failing students as somebody else's children, we will continue to undermine public schools' ability to successfully educate all children.

If the civil rights issues of the 1950s and 1960s were about equal *access*, the next generation of struggle in public education is about equal *success*. No big-city school system in the United States has yet figured out how to ensure that all students, particularly black and Latino, achieve at acceptable academic levels. While funding is not the only shortcoming, it is an important and solvable piece of the puzzle.

CHAPTER NINE

Fresh Air

IN DECEMBER 2000, MY FOUR-YEAR TERM on the Boston School Committee was coming to an end. I was just figuring out how things worked, how to weigh in. This was no time to step down.

John was settled into his new career as an elementary school teacher, providing me with additional inside information on the schools.

Ben was doing well in college in Chicago, while Jesse was a junior at Boston Latin School. Jesse didn't love the school the way Ben had, but it had the only sailing team in the Boston Public Schools, and he was its captain. When he brought home mediocre grades as a sophomore, John and I pressed him.

"Jesse, you know you can do better than that. Cs are not acceptable. You just whip through your homework. We need to see a little effort."

"Don't compare me to Ben," he would argue. "You need to understand that Ben is not a normal kid!" He'd then roll over on the sofa and change the television channel.

One day he described to me how his friends talked about their approach to barely getting by at Boston Latin. "We decided we'd be better off coming out at the bottom of the top, than the top of the bottom." Even the kids understood what was at stake—and the huge gap in opportunities in Boston's high schools.

Working on my new application to the mayor and school committee's nominating panel forced me to take stock. For all my inadequacies, I could point to some significant accomplishments, including the investment in additional supports to help students meet higher promotion standards, revisions to the promotion policy, and helping many parent and community groups better understand and work with the school system. The school committee was in the process of negotiating a new family and community engagement policy with the superintendent. I was in the middle of working with outside advocates to ensure that this new policy would include a new deputy superintendent position to give it visibility and status. I knew that my presence on the school committee lent it credibility with many outside advocates and parents who believed the committee was otherwise unresponsive.

The learning curve had been steep, and I was now on its other side. I believed I had more to contribute and was up to the challenge.

On New Year's Eve of 2000, I was sworn in to a second four-year term on the Boston School Committee. Ben was home for the holiday break, and the whole family joined me at the mayor's office for the formalities. I signed the large, musty city record, and we headed out to celebrate the new year.

This time around, I shook the mayor's hand with confidence as we left his office.

In my case for reappointment, I argued that school climate was a serious problem that needed attention. Too many policy initiatives got mired down because of a lack of trust between school leadership and staff; too many good ideas were put to premature death as a result of general cynicism and negativity. You can't mandate attitudes—this was something beyond a new policy initiative. I proposed that the school committee hold community forums as a way to bring disparate factions closer together on the issues at hand.

An earlier dialogue process run by the deputy superintendent had inspired my thinking. She had invited teachers, parents, and administrators together for discussion on a topic I no longer remember. What I did remember was the dozen chairs she arranged in a circle in the middle of the school cafeteria. Another couple dozen chairs were lined up in rows outside the circle. The arriving teachers looked around the cafeteria skeptically.

The deputy superintendent welcomed everybody and explained how the session would work. She then invited people into the inner circle to answer a set of questions on the topic at hand. The rules were that anybody in the audience could jump into one of the empty seats in the circle if they felt compelled to join the conversation.

You want us to do what? The idea of holding a conversation in a circle in front of an audience did not elicit enthusiasm on the part of the teachers.

After each question, the inner circle rotated out, and a new group of participants was invited in to discuss the deputy superintendent's next question. As people began to talk back and forth across the circle, they warmed up to the conversation and forgot they were being watched.

Afterwards, everybody departed with a lighter step, acknowledging how they had learned so much from listening to each other.

I also thought back to my meetings with the young people as part of my job with YouthBuild. Those high school dropouts, when given respect and responsibility, helped create stronger programs. The process of asking for their input also created a sense of ownership. These same young people, when in environments where decisions were in somebody else's hands, were quick to cast blame elsewhere for their own failure. So were our teachers.

The opportunity to participate pushed them all to think about solutions, not just problems. And having been part of the problem, they proposed solutions that were often more effective, created out of a deeper understanding of the obstacles.

In the Boston Public Schools, we were *disengaging* too many of the key groups with a stake in our public schools—students, parents, teachers, administrators, and community residents. This was no way to solve problems, and my experiences with the opposite approach affirmed the point.

I scheduled a time to meet with Liz, the school committee chair, to discuss my proposal for community forums. I had supported Liz's bid to become chair back in January 1998, impressed with her political sensibility and focus. Over time, however, my regard for her management style had shifted. If I thought committee members lacked interaction when I first was appointed, it dropped even further under her leadership.

Liz moved us through our agendas with an efficiency that left little space for debate. On nights when the Boston Symphony was performing, I could count on her getting us out the door not a minute past eight o'clock. If a committee member got long-winded during discussion of an agenda item, she would turn to them and peer down through her reading glasses, waiting for the slightest pause.

"Thank you, Mr. Arroyo. We need to move on."

I learned to avoid having Liz's reading glasses turned my way by limiting my comments to three on any given agenda item. I'd scratch my concerns on my agenda, circling and crossing out lines until I found the most important points I wanted to make. There was nothing wrong with managing the committee's time, and we all knew that our colleague Mr. Arroyo liked giving speeches. But I thought—perhaps naïvely?—that we were there to weigh in on the issues. Many agenda items went through our meetings with no discussion at all.

After most meetings, I left school committee headquarters feeling heated about the lack of debate. *What were we there for?* I believed it should be more than the ego gratification of being a public official. I also believed it should be our role to encourage broader participation in school policy decisions.

After one such meeting, I pulled Liz aside as we stepped down from the platform and grabbed our coats off the rack behind us. "Liz, I really think parent and community input could help move our agenda. They bring an important perspective to the issues."

I could detect Liz's discomfort when one of her shoulders lifted a couple of inches toward her ear. "I don't disagree that we should respond to concerns from the public. But the parents' job is to be there for their children, at home, and at their children's school." Her right shoulder edged up. She was not interested in parent advice on policy issues.

This conversation, which we were to repeat a number of times, infuriated me. And our relationship hadn't warmed up any since my reappointment. When we met to discuss my proposal to organize community forums, I was not optimistic about her likely response.

"I'm not against community input." Her right shoulder went up a couple of inches. "As long as you're willing to do the legwork." Liz put my proposal on the next school committee meeting agenda. I got the green light to proceed on the committee's behalf.

After so many lone votes against proposals that everybody else supported, I felt isolated and tended to operate independently. I had gotten used to that role, unfortunately. I only wished I could figure out how to sway my colleagues to my side. I had grown tired of staking my position and not seeing it change the outcome. Maybe it was the middle-child syndrome. My father often liked to tell how, when my siblings and I were children, I was always the one who went off by myself to do my own thing.

I didn't ask my colleagues to help with the community forums. They were curious enough to show up. Looking back, it is clear that I missed an opportunity to bring them in. It is also clear that this way of operating is one more way in which white people and our society in general reinforce an individualistic, competitive set of values. Go it alone; be the star—even if we might get a better outcome for everybody by working together.

I proposed that the first community forum series focus on student support—what middle school and high school students needed beyond academics in order to succeed. This was after higher graduation standards had been established, and one common refrain from high school staff was that students were coming in to high school unprepared. It was a setup for high schools to fail at their new, more stringent charge. I wanted the forums to explore shortcomings at both the middle and the high school levels that caused students to fall behind. I thought back to the Gavin School Politics Club, and I knew this was about more than what took place in the classroom.

As I began to lay the groundwork for the community forum series, a pleasant surprise arrived from unexpected quarters. A friend of the National Coalition of Education Activists offered her seaside summer house for our steering committee meetings. I had now been on the steering committee for two years. Our quarterly meetings had been a welcome respite, when committee members came together to figure out how to support our colleagues across the country struggling with the same challenges as mine back in Boston.

On a warm and sunny Friday afternoon in April 2000, I left work early for our weekend meeting. I drove by the bus station, Logan Airport, then neighboring Cambridge, squeezing steering committee colleagues into my two-door Honda. We headed out of Boston, toward a little peninsula south of Cape Cod, catching up on each other's children, the latest budget battles in Cincinnati, Gloria's trip to see how schools worked in Mexico. Our respective city lives and families and stresses receded as we drank in the fresh salt air.

By the time we got out of my car two hours later, we had caught our collective breath. We then became millionaires for the weekend, each claiming a bed from among the multiple bedrooms. The early arrivals had already made a group outing to the local grocery store for meal supplies. Flipchart paper filled one wall of the airy living room overlooking the ocean. The camaraderie provided a stark contrast to the cynicism and frustrations I left behind in Boston.

With the sun setting over the ocean, I tossed the dinner salad and listened to the stories of teachers from New Jersey and Portland. Surrounded by so much light and air, I opened my mind in a way that was barely possible back home. The African American and Puerto Rican parents and parent organizers on the steering committee spoke frankly about how they were treated by white parents and school administrators. I could hear them without the defensiveness that came from being the direct object of similar criticisms back home. I found hope in the good work being done in small pockets elsewhere.

My participation in this steering committee helped me to channel my anger and frustrations, as we sorted out common problems, identified topics for the upcoming newsletter, and debated themes for next year's annual conference. It also reinforced the idea that building relationships is critical to making change.

Back in Boston, I started planning the community forum series. I called on Karen, the director of an educational research institute at Northeastern University, to help design the sessions planned for that fall.

I had first met Karen in 1998, when a group of parents, including me, who shared frustrations with the citywide parent council decided to launch a new parent organizing coalition. The newly formed Boston Parent Organizing Network selected Karen's institute as its fiscal sponsor and home.

Karen, an African American woman with endless energy and a sharp intellect, had the right balance of credentials for the community forums. She was respected in both education and community circles. She had spent a number of years doing research on the impact of family engagement on student achievement. Karen could describe her findings in plain language that conveyed passion and commitment. Simultaneously warm and businesslike, she also was an excellent trainer and facilitator.

We designed the sessions to engage teachers, administrators, parents, students, and interested people from the community—people who rarely had the opportunity to talk with one another as equals. The goals were to broaden understanding of the problems and open up thinking about possible solutions across groups of people who generally viewed each other as adversaries. This seemed like the only way to build consensus among all the groups that were invested in our youth and in positions to make change happen. It could give everybody a role to play in the process.

I started appearing regularly at the school committee office downtown. This was quite different from my first term on the committee, when I disappeared out the door in discomfort as soon as I could.

I came bearing contact information and sample public service announcements for Boston's Spanish and Haitian radio stations, along with long lists of community organizations to be sent forum invitations. Churches, the gang unit of the police department, student support staff from the school department—I wanted everybody at the table. I kept reminding myself that this was not business as usual. The entire process required patience, as I showed up in the school committee office each week with yet another list of contacts, insisting that we pay for refreshments and child care.

The three school committee staff had their routines. On good days, they took my lists and instructions without complaint. On other days, one would remind me, "Ms. Naimark, have you forgotten that we have a committee meeting this week? We'll get to this when we can, but it won't be today."

I'm sure they were tempted to duck out the back door when they saw me walking toward their office from the sixth-floor elevator. I was on a mission to make sure that people turned out and that everybody felt welcome once they got to these forums.

The first forum was held in October 2001 at Northeastern University, a sprawling urban campus with easy access by both public transportation and car, a critical criterion for maximizing attendance. The dean of the university's education department was glad to support us by making the facilities available. I called the school committee staff almost hourly the day before the forum, needing assurance that there were proper signs posted at the door and inside the building so as not to reinvent my own first meeting experiences wandering around darkened school buildings.

Our meeting room was more elegant and comfortable than anything we could offer in a Boston school setting. Thinking of my experience with the NCEA board, I knew the setting could help put people in a more open frame of mind. I stood in the back, rehearsing my opening remarks to myself as people trickled into the room. The director of an after-school program thanked me for being invited.

"We never get a chance to talk directly with people from the schools! We've been trying forever. I'm so glad you're doing this."

Parents from Brighton, Mattapan, Jamaica Plain, and Dorchester added their names to the sign-in sheet at the table set up by the door. A couple of teens from the Mayor's Youth Council quietly slipped into seats in the back of the room.

Karen welcomed the audience on behalf of the university. I then framed the session.

"We have a very tough challenge facing us, and we need your help. As you know, we have raised the standards for promotion and graduation in the Boston Public Schools over the last few years. I think everybody would agree that we needed to change the way we did business—passing young people along every year and giving them diplomas that did not guarantee they had the basic skills needed to get along as adults did not do them any favors. But I'm not sure that we have really figured out how to adequately support our young people to be sure they have everything they need to reach the new, higher standards....

"We are holding these forums because we know that our students are capable of succeeding. We also know that they need a range of supports in their lives, and the Boston Public Schools have to be a partner to families, community groups, and others to be sure our children have the supports they need to succeed.... We are very clear that the BPS cannot do it alone, and neither can families. We need to work together."

Karen picked up from here, instructing people to divide into small groups for discussion. She handed out instructions that we had meticulously designed. Each group had to pick a person to record the discussion and another to act as timekeeper. They then had fifteen minutes to discuss the challenges to academic success and the supports needed to address these challenges. Small groups ended with instructions to prioritize the list of supports, identifying the most important ones to start with.

The room buzzed.

It was Karen's idea to end the session with pledge sheets photocopied on lavender paper. She looked at her watch and boomed, "Time to wrap up."

As people refocused toward the front of the room, Karen continued. "This session isn't just about talk, although that's important, too. We don't want anybody leaving here without making a personal commitment to be part of the solution to the problems our young people face."

I moved through the room on cue, handing out blank forms as Karen went on.

"I'd like everybody in this room to take a lavender pledge sheet and write down the ways you're willing to help out."

As soon as I got home that night, I flipped through the lavender papers.

A manager of after-school programs in Dorchester pledged to increase communication between his programs, schools, and parents.

A community health center manager pledged to increase the size and quality of the center's after-school programs.

A school staff person pledged to put together a program to help new immigrant students adapt to the new culture.

Parents pledged to be more involved with their children, participate in the parent council at their children's school, be more supportive of the teachers.

I'm going into detail here about how we organized these forums because one of the things I learned was that details mattered. To get people to the table who hadn't been there before, we needed to pay great attention to doing outreach that went beyond flyers in children's backpacks. To get everybody comfortable participating, we needed to be sure the signage on an unfamiliar college campus steered them to the meeting room on time and that the room and the greeters at the door were welcoming. We needed to make the rules of engagement explicit, so that those most familiar with the culture of meetings weren't the only ones who knew how to chime in.

We needed to actively counteract all the things large and small that the school system had done for years that sent people packing. It helped to have as forum cofacilitator a person of color who was respected in communities of color. Also helpful was my personal contacts with people of color who headed community agencies, asking for their assistance with outreach and encouraging their participation. In addition I made sure to recruit volunteers who looked like the mix of Boston Public School families to welcome forum participants on arrival.

Over 250 people attended that first forum series, a diverse group in terms of race, role, neighborhood, age, and more. A clear set of themes emerged. The school department needed to do a better job of integrating social supports with academic supports. After-school activities needed to be more widely available to young teens, and these programs needed to link back to what was being taught in school. Better communication between schools, families, and community organizations was needed. Lastly, adults needed to cultivate more meaningful and caring relationships with youth.

For each of these areas, specific strategies had been identified. These recommendations became a useful road map for everybody involved. A number of the recommendations were adopted by various participants and community agencies.

I felt a stirring of hope that maybe we really *could* turn around the alienating reputation of the Boston Public Schools. These forums and the new relationships they established held the possibility for traction. I could *taste* that possibility. Years later, when I had stepped down from the school committee, I could see some of the residual effect of these efforts. A budget for school-based family and community outreach staff was established and grew steadily for a number of years. Superintendent Payzant became more willing to engage parents and community residents in broader ways. One of his first moves in this direction was to hire Karen, my community forum coleader, as Boston's first deputy superintendent for family and community engagement.

But organizing the forum series took a lot out of me. It consumed every spare minute, and many more that I didn't have to spare, through the fall of 2001. By the time we had presented our findings, another new year had rolled around. Through the cold winter of 2002, I surveyed my commitments during my early morning runs. Could I assign a relative weight to each? What gave me energy, and what drained it away?

On the home front, I had dutifully dulled any sense of urgency as my means of emotional survival. My relationship with John was at a standstill. The distance between us had continued to widen over the years I was missing in action from family life. Every once in awhile, we went out for dinner and acknowledged the problem.

"We need to be more honest with each other about how we're feeling," I would venture. Away from the distractions and momentarily relaxed by a shared bottle of wine, John would agree. Once in awhile, I believed he understood my distance. I was on the fence about whether our marriage was still giving me what I needed in a relationship, terrified to say it aloud. Too much was at stake: our family life, the well-being of our two sons.

Had I outgrown this relationship? I often wondered.

"You're like a bird," he said as he held his hand in a gentle, open cup facing upward, "ready to fly away." We both acknowledged how I couldn't have become all that I was becoming without his nurturing support over the years we had been together. I looked at his cupped hand, waiting for him to let go. And I realized in that moment that this was my decision to make, not his.

When the community forum series ended, Jesse was a senior in high school. He had managed his way through the academic pressure of sophomore and junior years, and he was now on cruise control at school. Between his after-school job at a neighborhood grocery store and his social life, he wasn't home much. John and I had fewer parental logistics to coordinate.

It was time to make my move.

"I need to move out," I announced to John one evening in early spring of 2002. I needed some time apart to think about what I needed to stabilize my emotional life.

I was terrified by what these five words might unleash.

We sat facing each other in our shared office space on the third floor of the house we had called home for over twenty years. Jesse was downstairs doing homework, Ben off at college. I had already arranged to move into a small attic apartment just up the street that belonged to a friend who had moved to New York City.

John's hands balled up into fists as he railed at me about the invest-ment in our marriage, how it was all lost now. I had never seen him so mad. I kept my eyes on his fists. *Was he going to hit me?* I had never known him to be physically violent, but we were now in uncharted terrain.

We began shouting at each other, unleashing emotions that had been bottled up for years. John didn't make any physical moves against me, but the commotion brought Jesse upstairs.

"What's going on up here?"

"I'm moving out—I don't know for how long. This is not about you, Jesse. I love you—I hope you know that. I just need some time to myself."

This was a place I had never wanted to be, but I saw no other way out.

During the next few months, I stopped at home only to pick up mail and check in with Jesse. And I kept up appearances at school committee, at work; I didn't even tell my parents I had moved out. I spent any unbooked time alone, listening to music, writing in my journal, staring at the walls. I scheduled a weeklong vacation.

Finally, slowly, I started to feel lonely, to miss John. He was right: we had both invested a lot in our marriage. No, it wasn't perfect. But as I al-ways told Ben and Jesse, life isn't perfect. In the balance, I realized that I cared deeply for John and valued our relationship more than I imagined. It worked more than it didn't—by a long shot.

After three months of living in the apartment up the street, I picked up the phone and dialed home. "John, I want to talk. Can we meet for din-ner?" We met at a neighborhood restaurant. An awkward date with my husband—how strange.

"I'd like to come home," I told him. He had waited patiently, never questioning his commitment to me. And I realized that my struggles weren't created or caused by my marriage. The only place I was going to find a better balance was somewhere deep inside myself.

I got to the other side of the turmoil in my home life, but it hadn't re-duced my external commitments. Leaving my day job was not an option. Despite John's move from a sometimes tenuous nonprofit to a more stable teaching job, our household still needed two incomes. Yet my new job had become a significant source of stress.

I had left YouthBuild when the opportunity came up to head the Success Measures Project, a promising new national model for documenting impact in community development. The project was sponsored by the Development Leadership Network, a national membership organization of people working in community development who wanted to connect their work to larger social justice organizing. Within months, the board of directors had asked me to become executive director of this previously all-volunteer organization, and I had accepted. By now I thought I was more fearless and less naïve. One of my first moves as director was to work with a couple of board members to put anti-racism work front and center on our agenda. This was a bold move, attracting new members and generating new dialogue around the country. It also became the beginning of the organization's undoing.

We held a conference, Undoing Racism in Community Development, in Phoenix that same spring, 2002.

The conference was a success, but significantly underenrolled. Staff enthusiasm had clouded our perspective about how broad the appeal would be for this topic. By the end of the conference, we owed the conference center thousands of dollars for unfilled rooms we had committed to in our contract. For a small nonprofit, this was a heavy burden.

The organization's member services coordinator spent hours on the phone trying to negotiate our bill down to something we could manage. I listened to her on the phone from my desk on the other side of the office partition. She was *tough*, I thought, appreciating that I didn't have to take on this thankless task myself. She succeeded in trimming the outstanding bill significantly. I tossed and turned at night, my thoughts consumed by how to cover payroll.

The organization also used its new focus on racism to look inward. My small staff of four included two African American women and a young Latina high school student who worked part-time. The inward look included a commitment to be honest about how we all *felt* about our work, about the racial and power dynamics that rarely are acknowledged aloud in organizations. We sat in our small conference room for staff meetings, and I increasingly felt cornered by the things my staff said.

"Your report to funders about our dialogues across the country needs a broader perspective."

None of the other staff had wanted to review it when I first drafted it and asked for their input. Now they were blaming me for not getting broader input.

"You're too controlling of the board meetings. If people have topics they want to bring up, you need to be more respectful."

My frustration with board meetings was that they never seemed to reach resolution. I couldn't even get an annual budget passed because the meetings went off topic so much.

Under pressure, I defaulted to withdrawal and defensiveness. When the African American staff pointed out how I was reacting, I was stunned.

They described my behavior in terms that sounded like all the worst bosses I had ever had. But they hadn't *known* these bosses. They couldn't be making this up. These were issues I cared deeply about, and I couldn't figure out how to solve them. If I left this job, it would prove my lack of commitment.

White people always have the option of leaving when the issue of race gets uncomfortable, while people of color don't have that choice, my staff and board members of color reminded me regularly.

I couldn't figure out how to make this organization work. Day-to-day tension between me and other staff was palpable when I arrived at work. My excitement about leading had turned to horror. My dream job had turned into a nightmare.

As I muddled through this mess, my nighttime and weekend thoughts edged perilously close to suicidal. *If I can't figure out how to address racism within my own small organization, I must be an impostor.* At best, I felt like a totally ineffective leader. I sat on the edge of my bed and cried. John hovered over me helplessly, without a clue how to pull me back from the abyss.

I knew intellectually that my reactions had as much to do with the stress of my workload as with the specific problems in front of me. If I could just find a way to remove some of the relentless pressure, I might be able to think more clearly and get through this—somehow.

I decided it was time to resign from the NCEA steering committee. I had been recruited to serve as cochair two years earlier, and that commitment now seemed the most expedient to sever. I never felt able to give the organization the time and attention it deserved. The commitment hung around my neck, getting heavier with each passing month.

My last steering committee meeting at the mansion on the ocean south of Boston in the spring of 2002 was bittersweet. Other board members were equally involved in local education organizing, many, like me, doing the work in addition to their paid jobs. They knew enough about burnout to understand and respect my decision when I announced my resignation. A few committee members went off during a break, returning with a yoga starter kit that they presented to me as they wished me well.

It was only when I got some distance that I understood how the stress I felt was related to my decision to take on racism. I saw that white people inevitably go through some version of emotional upheaval as they learn to see the world in new ways. Through my school committee and parent organizing roles, I had gradually learned to speak up about racial injustices. I had learned the importance of white people naming concerns that, paradoxically, are easily dismissed when raised by people of color. It took a deeper level of understanding to see how white privilege works, to hold up the mirror and realize that I was part of the problem, even as I worked to name and address racism. This was a hard pill to swallow.

At my day job, we had brought in anti-racist training for all staff and board members that included an analysis of the benefits of racism to white people. Before this training, I was convinced that I was on the same team as the people of color with whom I battled the schools. In a sense, I was.

But in another sense, I continued to benefit from the present institutional arrangements. Because of my Jewish upbringing and my family's frequent financial strains, I had not identified as someone from the majority culture, someone who benefited from unearned privilege. Once I understood that in fact I did benefit from being white, I had to rethink who I was. I had to toss out and reinvent my relationship to my world. I had to rewind decades of tapes in my mind and find the contradictions, like my father's VA mortgage that got us through tough times, which other people's fathers were denied because of the color of their skin. Or the ease with which my sons got into Boston Latin School, as a result of their middle-class experiences that allowed them to do well on standardized tests and the unquestioning support of their abilities and potential by the world around them.

Reexamining all of these things was not an easy process. But once you see how it works, you can't *not* see it. The emotional strain I had been under certainly had something to do with the weight of all my commitments. But it had as much to do with the disorientation of learning to accept that I benefited from my white skin as I moved through life.

* * *

After resigning from the NCEA steering committee, I began planning the next community forum series for the Boston Public Schools, this time focused on the achievement gap. State-mandated high-stakes testing was going into effect in the coming school year, with diplomas going only to the students who passed the test by June 2003. Based on historical data, it was no secret who was most likely to fail: the black and Latino students whose aggregate test scores were still consistently half the average scores of their white and Asian peers. Doing nothing to address this gap amounted to silent complicity with the status quo.

On this topic, I knew that the youth voice had the first chance of shaking the adults out of our comfort zones. I thought back to my earlier work with YouthBuild youth from across the country. They understood what was at stake, weren't afraid to name it, and were equally clear about possible solutions.

I enlisted the Boston Student Advisory Council, the director of a university-based program for Latino teens, youth and parent organizers, and a few sympathetic high school headmasters to help out. This time around, the superintendent assigned several of his deputies to lend their support as well. I had learned something since the earlier community forums about building a team, asking for help, and sharing the work.

The evening of the first forum, Superintendent Payzant found himself coming down with a bad cold. It was November, the beginning of the New England cold season. He phoned me at work that afternoon. "I'm afraid I'm going to have to beg off from tonight's forum. I'd love to be there, but I need to take care of this cold. I've asked Manuel to open the session for me. I hope you don't mind. I'm sure he'll do fine."

The deputy superintendent he asked to pinch-hit was a native Spanish speaker, a good move since this first forum was being held at English High School in Jamaica Plain, where we expected a good turnout of Spanish-speaking people. Manuel was one of the younger, newer deputy superintendents, earnest but still somewhat untested.

All went well as I welcomed the audience and outlined expectations for the evening. Then Manuel started talking. Yes, he was bilingual, and people appreciated that he delivered his opening remarks in two languages. But the words coming out of his mouth weren't right at all.

"You parents need to be involved in your children's education. We can't do it alone in the schools. You have to send your kids to school every day. You need to check their homework and show up at school for the open houses...." Manuel lapsed into a lecture, scolding the audience for the lack of parent involvement in their children's education.

Sitting in the front row of the auditorium, I tried to be discreet as I turned around and craned my neck to gauge the audience reaction. Maybe it was just me, but the tone of his voice seemed awfully patronizing. And he didn't know when to stop. This was supposed to be the speech that made people feel good about being there, let them know we were doing business differently with these forums and were ready to welcome their ideas. We had a good turnout, and all I could think of was damage control.

We went on to get some useful input from the audience, but my own thoughts were focused on how to approach Manuel and his boss about what had happened and why it was problematic. It didn't take long for my opening to appear. The parent organizer from one of the community organizations who had brought people out to the forum approached me a couple weeks later.

"Somebody's got to do something about that deputy superintendent. I worked hard to get people out to that forum, and they felt so insulted...."

That was all I needed. The next time I saw him, I conveyed the message. "Manuel, I wanted to give you some feedback I got about the forum. I was really glad you could open up the session. But I heard from one of the parent organizers who brought out a group of parents that they felt like you were lecturing at them. You know, those parents who showed up are the ones who *are* involved. I don't think they are the ones who needed a reminder about that."

I knew he wasn't going to argue with a school committee member. He was too new to the system and too polite. "I didn't mean to come across that way," he responded. I wanted to believe him and hoped the message sank in.

I tell this story because it happens all the time. Those of us in positions of power in particular so easily come across as patronizing without even knowing it. We usually mean well, and frequently we don't have a clue how our words are received. Misinterpretations are amplified when the power relationship between the speaker and listener is unequal and when race puts up barriers of mistrust. This was one of the things that happened in my day job, when I crashed and burned in the face of my African American staff. I didn't *mean* to dismiss their input. I spent many staff meetings arguing about this. At some point, I came to understand that it didn't matter what I intended. I had to respect their interpretation, honor their feelings, value their perspective, and, ultimately, change my behavior.

Despite the rough start, the second forum series attracted a diverse audience of 220 people over the course of three sessions. The student participants were the stars, articulating problems and solutions with the credibility of people who lived it every day.

The three sessions each opened with a student panel. My planning team wanted the students' experiences to be the starting point for discussion. We had asked various high schools to choose students to sit on each session's opening panel. Most of the students were African American or Latino, representative of the majority of students in the school system. This was the first year that high school students were required to pass the new state tests, the Massachusetts Comprehensive Assessment System, MCAS for short, in order to graduate. The students didn't mince words.

One student said: "I believe that MCAS could be a great test, but with MCAS there were supposed to be a lot of things that were supposed to come along with the test, and I've yet to see that. I go to South Boston High, and last week we learned our math curriculum on a window shade with a projector that was broke. I'm a freshman, I'm new to that school, and I'm fresh coming out of middle school, and there's a lot of things that I have to adapt to. But also I have to think about MCAS for next year, taking MCAS classes this year, but sometimes I think, why should I take it if I have to learn my math curriculum on a projector on a broken old window shade? Who cares about me? Who cares about why I am here learning math off a window shade?"

The students never failed to wake up the audience and keep the conversation real. They reminded us that it was their academic success at stake. Their perspectives were nuanced and honest, with lots of heated debate about the extent to which low achievement was the students' responsibility or the schools'. While some leaned one way or the other, most communicated that, in the end, it was a shared responsibility, as stated by one student:

> I don't think it's necessarily effective to only blame teachers. I think that the problem with the Boston Public School system is that we blame either the schools, or the teachers, or the students solely. I think that it's actually all three—the teachers, the students, and the school system need to be improved.... Every single part needs to be held accountable to some degree.... Students need to do their homework. We shouldn't only look at students as victims of the Boston Public School system, because we are not victims of the school system—we're just all products of it. Teachers need to be more encouraged, and the school system needs to provide more resources, and all together we can have a better Boston Public School system. ...It's a collective whole. We need to focus on how we can improve all three so we can have a better future for all of us.

For anybody inclined to negatively stereotype students, this statement by an African American student dispelled that inclination. She sat at the table on the stage in her tight jeans and oversized gold earrings, looking a lot like her peers, many of whom were being failed by their schools. She left no doubt that young people like her had much to contribute to solving the problems of failing schools.

Students from some of the lowest-performing high schools in the city spoke with clarity about the connection between effective teaching and learning:

> The way I see it, teachers need to speak in a way they can get through to the students. You can't think that every single student has the same learning style, because we don't. With some of my friends, I know they get distracted and sometimes they try to distract me, but that doesn't work.... You can't get through to someone if you're teaching the way you want to teach. You need to teach where the students are going to listen to you. You need to bond with the students, or else they're just

going to be, 'Oh, I don't want to do it.' They're going to distract other people, and that's how your learning community or the school is just going to go down because they don't get it—that's why they're not paying attention."

The student panelists were equally forthcoming with praise for what worked in their schools:

The reason why Mr. ___'s English class is going well, and I think it's the most effective English class I've ever taken, is because he takes really challenging books and makes us all relate to them in some way or form. We read *Approaching the Koran*. We read Plato's *Republic*, and we're reading Dante's *Inferno* right now. I think all of those books are college-level books. Our English class is not tiered. It's not advanced. You can decide to take honors English within that class by doing extra work.... You can meet this teacher after school every single day. He does a real good job because he has a 'refuse to fail' English program."

What came out loud and clear was that high expectations, motivation, and support were a shared responsibility of students, families, and schools—and all were falling short.

Students spoke passionately about the need for improved understanding and respect for them and their peers by school staff. Jewel, an outspoken young woman of color who went on to become the student representative on school committee a few years later, said it bluntly, referring to school staff who failed to understand their own shortcomings in dealing with students, "These people have cultural deficit disorder."

People were finally having real conversations about the dismal failure of the system with black and Latino students. This is not a phenomenon unique to Boston. In fact, Boston had made better progress than most other big-city school districts. But even at Boston's rate of improvement, it would be decades before students of color might achieve at the same levels as white students. As Jewel pointed out, the challenge was as much about attitude and understanding as it was about curriculum and testing.

An often-cited experiment demonstrated clearly how attitudes and expectations affect student achievement. In 1968, in response to the assassination of Martin Luther King Jr., a white Iowa elementary school teacher decided to teach her all-white third grade class a lesson in discrimination. She separated the students by eye color, informing those with blue eyes of

their superiority and those with brown eyes of their inferiority. She then proceeded with class, reminding each group of their superiority or inferiority
along the way. The next day, she reversed roles. And what she found was that
the students performed according to their respective group assignments—
even when they were switched from day to day.

This experiment has been repeated many times since, with adults as
well as children. And the results have been consistent. Research since has
named this phenomenon "stereotype threat," a pattern where people who
have been negatively stereotyped are likely to perform poorly when they
believe they will be evaluated according to those stereotypes. In short, expectations make a huge difference to behavior and outcomes.

* * *

As we wrapped up the second series of school committee community
forums, an invitation arrived in my home mail to Ernesto's wedding. Ben's
old friend from elementary school would be the first of his close friends to
get married. Ben, now twenty-one years old, flew home from college in
Chicago to attend. John, Ben, and I looked forward to reconnecting with
Ernesto and his family after a few years' gap.

"I can't believe Ernesto's getting married," Ben sighed.

Ben had spent the last three years taking full advantage of all that the
University of Chicago had to offer. He identified an array of travel stipends
and fellowships and pursued them all. He did research one winter in Chile,
got a paid internship the next summer in Mexico City, and organized
Habitat for Humanity trips to Nicaragua during spring breaks.

After their paths had diverged as teenagers, Ernesto had gone from
one of the lowest-performing middle schools in Boston to Madison Park,
Boston's vocational-technical high school, with one of the highest dropout
rates in the city. By Ernesto's junior year, he had completed all of his
graduation course requirements, and a guidance counselor suggested he
enroll in community college. Then that guidance counselor left, and that
was the end of any guidance for Ernesto.

By his senior year of high school, Ernesto was bored. He was president
of the student council, active in the chess club and martial arts club. Other
than that, all he needed to do was show up. His girlfriend got pregnant

that year. After that, child support and feeding a family became his top priority.

When Ernesto sent the invitation to his high school graduation, John had taken off from work to attend. We knew this was likely to be the end of Ernesto's formal education. After graduation, he went right to work at Home Depot. He continued to treat his jobs like schooling, learning everything he could and rapidly getting promoted. Over the next few years, he held a series of management positions in national retail stores.

When asked years later about the lack of support for going to college, Ernesto's quick response was, "This is the part that bothers me to this day." Despite his success in retail management, he went on, "I'm still looking for that sense of accomplishment."

Looking back at the lives of these two young men, it was clear to me that their respective sense of options resided in two different worlds, two different trajectories, determined by an accident of birth and cemented by a series of circumstances.

For me, the wedding was bittersweet. On the drive home, I finally voiced a thought that had circled through my mind many times over the years. "Whenever I think about you and Ernesto, Ben, I've always thought that your lives are the perfect examples of how racism and white privilege work."

Ben's response was immediate. "I know what you mean; I've said almost the same thing. Ernesto was always so much smarter than me. He always did better than me on math tests."

What Ben didn't need to say out loud was how much narrower Ernesto's life options had become over the years, while Ben's were forever expanding in possibilities. When I met Ernesto recently to talk about this book, he confided that he had always wanted to go to the Massachusetts Institute of Technology, the world-renowned university just across the river from Boston. MIT had recently started to post some of their courses online, and Ernesto was following them.

Our high schools across the United States are full of Ernestos: smart children whose opportunities progressively narrow as they grow up, through decisions made by adults based, consciously or unconsciously, on race and class.

CHAPTER TEN

School Assignment Redux

WHITE, MIDDLE-CLASS FAMILIES WHO HAD CHOICES about where to send their children began to return to the Boston Public Schools through the 1990s. By 2003, the trickle was a steady flow.

Even with Boston's nagging failure rate, the school system had made significant progress during a decade of steady leadership under Superintendent Tom Payzant that coincided with my tenure on school committee. Up until the dismal spring of 2002, annual budgets had grown most years. Learning standards ensured greater consistency in curriculum across the city. The large district high schools had been divided into smaller learning communities, with some showing positive results. Inequities still existed, in both resources and academic outcomes. The results were still skewed in favor of white students, but a significant number of schools were showing strong results.

As enrollment swelled, the city launched an ambitious building campaign. By the summer of 2003, Boston had completed the construction of three new schools. All were located in communities of color that had shortages of public school seats. The ribbon cutting for the Orchard Gardens K-8 School brought together the neighborhood activists and school department and city officials who had made it happen.

The vision for this school had been created by residents of the adjacent public housing development. When funding for new schools was first announced, Orchard Gardens residents set up a committee to create a plan for the school they knew was going to be built down the street. The school committee was soliciting proposals for the new schools and accepted their plan. This was a first in many decades: public housing residents having their own new school. The school was to be overseen jointly by the school department and a board of trustees comprised of one-third school staff, one-third parents, and one-third community residents. The excitement was palpable, and the school attracted significant external funding.

Delight filled the air as public officials and community residents toured the building on that August morning. The library had high windows, providing a wide corner view of Boston's downtown financial district two miles away, as if to say, *This can be yours!* Every classroom had a full complement of new textbooks and a telephone that enabled teachers to communicate with the outside world. The halls were bright and clean. There was a dance studio with floor-to-ceiling mirrors. There were two art studios and a music studio, each ready to receive students with all the necessary equipment and supplies.

"This is as good as any suburban school!" said one city official to me as we moved through the well-stocked library.

Why shouldn't it be? I wondered.

Trustees and neighborhood residents were hopeful that at last the children in the adjacent community would have access to the quality education that had proved so elusive for so long. The following years, however, were to prove otherwise.

The Orchard Gardens K-8 School lost its first principal within a few short and contentious months of its opening in the fall of 2003. The second principal lasted through the school's second year, but not without conflict, suffering health problems, and ultimately taking a leave of absence. The third principal lasted one year. By then, the school was losing a full one-third of its teaching staff every year. By year four, external resources were dwindling, and the school had lost its appeal to the energetic young teachers it had originally attracted. It consistently ranked in the bottom 10 percent of all elementary schools in Massachusetts. At one point it had the distinction of being the lowest-performing school in the state.

The school's fourth principal began to stabilize the school. In 2006, for the first time, Orchard Gardens met federal "adequate yearly progress" in all categories designated by No Child Left Behind. Those first few years of significant financial investment had not ensured educational success; stable leadership was what began to make a difference. The school was a case study that money alone can't buy academic success.

The Orchard Gardens School's promise remained illusive through its first few years because of the turnover in leadership. Other schools in Boston were threatened by a proposed change in student assignment policy.

As white, middle-class families began to fill seats again at some of the system's better schools, political pressure increased on the school committee and the mayor to return to neighborhood schools. A 1999 federal lawsuit that resulted in the lifting of racial quotas in student assignment had created a new opening. Federal courts across the country were systematically rejecting the need for student assignment policies to address racial inequities.

By the fall of 2003, Liz phoned committee members one by one to test the waters in off-the-record conversations. At least a few of us insisted that if we were going to consider any changes to student assignment, we needed to do it with broad public input. Despite nearly three decades of distance since the original federal court order handed down in 1975 to desegregate the schools, we knew that student assignment was still a hot-button issue. It was the proxy for issues of school quality, equity, and the state of racism in our city.

In January 2004, the Boston School Committee launched a series of community meetings, focus groups, and surveys to gain broad input on the issue. The first round focused on listening to people's desires and concerns, and sharing information about the current status of school assignment, with a second round planned to get feedback to various options for change to student assignment. A separate committee of community representatives was established to take the lead in this process, in part to take the heat off of school committee. We also hoped this would broaden the circles of engagement and, in turn, give the process a level of credibility often lacking in school committee.

I wanted to believe that the committee had learned something about better engagement processes from the community forums I had organized.

As meetings were called to order in various neighborhoods across the city, professional facilitators did their best to explain the complicated data on student assignment. A meeting at the Murphy School in Dorchester packed the cafeteria one evening. A group of mostly white parents had come out in full force to weigh in for returning to neighborhood schools.

Participants sat at round lunchroom tables attempting to absorb the meaning of the many multicolored maps and charts displayed on a stand before them.

I stood back behind one table, observing. A few minutes into the presentation, one Murphy School father interrupted the facilitator. "You expect us to believe this information? It's common knowledge that student assignment is rigged. If you know the right people you can get into the school you want."

I decided to weigh in on this one.

"Maybe that used to be the case, but it's not any more."

"Yeah, right." He rolled his eyes.

At another forum, several parents shouted down the facilitators before they got to the data at all.

"Excuse me, but do you know that my child's school has broken windows in the library that haven't been fixed in years?"

Another parent stood up before the first had barely finished her question.

"I know this forum is supposed to be about student assignment. But before you go moving my kids around, you need to do something about the disrespect of the staff throughout this school system."

These forums were a rare opportunity to vent, and people took full advantage.

The school committee received a surge of emails. One such email from a white parent made clear his analysis of failing schools in communities of color in Boston:

"Boston has quality schools.... Just because a Roxbury or Dorchester school does not have overall high scores on standardized tests does not mean that it is not a quality school, it means that many children in that school are not getting the parental support at home in order to achieve at school."

Many other white parents echoed similar sentiments at the community meetings and in writing.

My own experiences led to a very different analysis. The court intervention in the 1970s came only after a full decade of pleas from black leaders. Boston had a long history of public officials blatantly ignoring the needs of children of color, despite clear evidence of inequitable resource distribution based on race. I had also met too many parents of color who did all the right things to support their children, only to see that they still did not succeed on par with their white peers. This was not about lack of support on the part of the parents. It was about a school system that persistently treated them differently, embedded in a larger society that did not provide the opportunities afforded white, middle-class families.

At the student assignment meetings, parents of color had a perspective that sharply diverged from the white parents, and they organized a group called Work-4-Quality Schools. Their concern was clear: A disproportionately high percentage of schools designated as underperforming based on standardized test scores was in predominantly black and Latino neighborhoods. If Boston were to move to neighborhood schools, it would be the black and Latino children living in these neighborhoods who would have no choice but to attend the worst schools.

As far as the argument that lack of parent involvement was the problem with underperforming students, the group pointed out that there was no evidence to suggest that being closer to a school would lead to increased parent participation.

Issues of race came to a head at the hearing in West Roxbury, a white, working-class and middle-class neighborhood and the least integrated neighborhood of the city. The auditorium was standing room only. A white supporter of the Work-4-Quality group walked up to the microphone set up in the aisle and voiced his concern about loss of opportunity for children of color if Boston returned to neighborhood schools.

A white city councilor seated in the auditorium leapt to her feet in response and shouted, "I grew up in public housing. I understand the problems, and I'm tired of hearing everybody blame the schools for everything." She was tired of hearing about racial disparities, about schools not working for children of color. She finished her statement with a vehement "Get over it!"

A white parent at that hearing was equally incensed, with a different take on the issues than the city councilor. "You people think all of us in West Roxbury are racists. You don't understand! The racists were the ones who moved out thirty years ago! We're the ones who stayed! If people want the quality they think we have in West Roxbury, they can move here!"

I shook my head as I thought about the community organizing job I had held a few years earlier in Roslindale, the next neighborhood over from West Roxbury. Roslindale had just begun to see an influx of Latino and black families at the time I was working there. My job was with a community coalition charged to take the pulse of the community and develop plans for improved coordination among community agencies. As I met with various groups throughout the community, a local Catholic priest tipped me off to the widespread practice of real estate agents in this part of the city routinely steering families of color away from West Roxbury and into the adjoining neighborhoods instead.

I had tucked the information away in my head, and now I wondered why I hadn't acted on it at the time. I suspected that the West Roxbury parent inviting families of color to move to her neighborhood had no awareness of such practices. She was also unlikely to know that the real estate practice of racial steering was well documented across the country, going back many decades.

The parents who came forward during these public hearings of 2004 were children themselves when the schools were forced by the courts to integrate in the 1970s. Some were still smarting from their experiences of that earlier era. Others who came forward this time around had not grown up in Boston. Personal experience with the original desegregation effort was not a prerequisite to personal attachment to the issues it represented.

No amount of evidence or arguments moved the white parents who were bent on returning to neighborhood schools. In reaction to the Work-4-Quality group, they formed a Walk-2-School group. This group was confident about its members' ability to go into any school—preferably in the neighborhood in which they lived—and make it work. Their argument was "Just give us our schools. We can make them quality. Quality comes from hard work, not just money."

The Work-4-Quality group did not have this confidence.

The debate throughout these hearings was both passionate and for the most part civil. This alone was significant, in a city where all politics—not just school politics—has historically been a blood sport. It showed that residents were capable of disagreeing and still respecting divergent points of view—to a point. And it showed the young people served by the schools that the adults could engage constructively and talk out their differences, even when their side didn't "win." Compared to the violence that had engulfed the city over these same issues a generation earlier, this in itself could be viewed as a victory.

Both groups willingly acknowledged that they were committed to working toward the same goal: high-quality public schools for all children in Boston. However, there was a vast difference of opinion about what it would take to get there. What unfolded was very different analyses by each of these groups, based on very different sets of experiences—not unlike the different perspectives and experiences I had encountered in my years of meeting with parent groups across the city.

The unspoken assumptions of each group were about how they understood and experienced their access to the institutions of power in Boston. The Work-4-Quality group, a racially diverse coalition led by people of color, did not believe they had the ability to walk into any school and be heard. They were not about to limit their children's schooling options until there was evidence that all neighborhoods had equitable access to high-quality schools.

The result of these hearings was to leave student assignment alone.

As I saw the differences—and similarities—in views emerge from groups like these over the years, I became convinced that racial integration wasn't the sole goal. The original federal lawsuit in Boston was about ensuring an equitable, high-quality education for children of color. Integration was the means, not the end. There is tremendous value in integration insofar as it enables children to interact and better understand each other's cultures, experiences, and perspectives. But integration without an explicit assurance of quality and equity wasn't going to fix our troubled public schools. And poor quality, inequitable schools weren't going to get fixed until those who experienced them had the power to make change.

CHAPTER ELEVEN

Reflections in the
Rearview Mirror

LIKE MOST CHILDREN, MINE TOOK THEIR UPBRINGING FOR GRANTED
and accepted their parents' choices at face value—as just the way things
were. Little did they know at the time how few white, middle-class children were exposed to the sometimes rough-and-tumble classrooms, sometimes dangerous school bus rides, and often arbitrary policies of big-city
public schools.

It was only as young adults that Ben and Jesse learned from their peers
that something was amiss in the education they received.

"Your parents sacrificed you to their political beliefs!" was the outraged
reaction Ben reported when he went off to the University of Chicago. For
the first time in his life, he was surrounded by other white, middle- and
upper-class overachievers like him. Jesse reported a variation on the same
reaction a few years later. This was the response of their peers in the wider
world on learning that their parents had sent them to the Boston Public
Schools.

Only a few people said it directly, but an underlying question was,
How could we allow them to be the only white kids? This idea frightened
many white people, who knew very little about big-city public schools beyond what they read in the newspaper or saw on TV.

These critics didn't focus on the strengths of diversity, only the dangers. John and I may have taken some risks in the parenting and schooling
decisions we made. But we never doubted that the power of all the experiences surrounding our sons' upbringings was overwhelmingly positive in
the balance.

Ben tossed off the comments with a scornful roll of his eyes as we sat at our kitchen table during his first college break. "They act as if I was lucky to come out alive! That's so ridiculous."

He learned his lessons well, I thought smugly.

There were, in fact, times during his childhood that I felt lucky that he came out alive. A decade later, I was reassured that those were not the overriding childhood memories he carried with him into adulthood.

Jesse was more casual as a young adult about these challenges to his upbringing. Possibly this was because he moved into the larger world not through an exclusive college but by moving to San Diego with friends right after high school. His first experiences in this new world were filled with a wider variety of people than Ben's: working people of all ages, from the grocery bagger with the name tag proudly proclaiming his twenty years on the job to his middle-aged boss, a Deadhead who still packed up his van to follow rock concerts across Southern California. Jesse was quick to notice racism in his co-workers and new friends in San Diego. "I can't believe the things these guys say. They have so little understanding."

If there is one thing I have learned over the years, it is that much racism is based on ignorance on the part of white people. Most white people do not see themselves as racist. Yet we continue to do and say things that offend people of color, largely because of our limited or complete lack of exposure to people of color. We also continue to think of ourselves as nonracial, as if white is not a racial identity. As long as we treat white as the unspoken norm, our views of people of color will remain stuck as "the other." This basic frame of reference limits our ability to fully value people and cultures different from our own.

Neither John nor I have any apologies for or regrets about how we raised our two sons. We also know that this exposure would have been possible in very few places, among them our local public schools.

Both Ben and Jesse readily acknowledge the value of their educational experience, in all of its strengths and challenges. As Ben reviewed draft chapters for this book, he added the following sentence to the end of one of my descriptions of him and Jesse: "As they grew older, they appreciated more and more the 'risks,' real and imagined, that we took." I couldn't have said it better myself.

Ben has followed closely in my footsteps, building on the interests in community and democracy that emerged during his college years, and I'm proud of him.

It's Jesse who keeps me from becoming too smug. Still independent-minded, he is more provocative when I ask him to reflect back on his schooling and talk about issues of race. He is grateful for the decisions John and I made and the values we imbued in him. He also lives up to the spirit of independence with which we raised him—or was it his red hair that made him a contrarian?

"There's another side to the story," he says. "I rarely hear people like you say that others need to take responsibility for themselves. Any situation, you get out of it what you take out of it. What I got out of it was that I understand that most situations have a lot to give. Even in the schools that have problems, you don't have to be involved in the problems.

"Once I got to Latin School, I had a lot of friends outside of that school who were from really lousy situations. As teens, they got into lots of trouble. I never understood what drove it. It was like self-destruction. They were perfectly smart, but that's what they were surrounded by. It was like they were trying to screw themselves up. If some kid's in a gang and wants to go rob people on Saturday night, I feel like people like that need to take responsibility to do something with themselves besides live up to crappy stereotypes."

He refers to his friend Jared, who attended Hyde Park High School, one of the lowest-performing high schools in Boston at the time. The school had full four-year scholarships available that didn't get used. Boston University provided these scholarships to qualifying students from every high school in Boston. Jesse believes that part of the problem is that there are too many kids who think, "That's not for me," and don't take advantage of the opportunities available to them. He goes on to bring his analysis even closer to home.

"In some ways, you white lefties perpetuate the problem by creating this very narrow group of people who think they are the champions of change. This doesn't always help. [People in] poorer communities look at you like, who the hell are you? The broader issue is that there is a societal rift between rich white people and poor black people. It's race, and it's also economics.

"When you can't even begin to relate to people who are different from you, how are you ever going to change them? Too many liberals can't even do that. What really needs to happen is that people who have made it from poor communities need to go back because they are the ones who can make the change."

There is truth in Jesse's words.

But I'm not ready to leave it at that, as if we white, middle-class people have no responsibility or role to play. When I press him on the power differential between black and white, he acknowledges that it exists. He understands there are historically embedded reasons why some black people don't take responsibility and that their collective ability to make change is not the same as us "white lefties." He remembers back to an experience in high school:

"When I was a senior in high school, doing my community service project, I went to six or eight homes, mostly in the projects, to help kids get their computers set up. I remember walking up to the McCormack projects in Southie. I parked my car and walked up to the building. There's trash everywhere. The grass is half dead. The paint's peeling off of everything that's painted. There's old Tonka trucks scattered in the dirt. The yard wasn't even grass; it was just dirt. If this is what I came home to every day—oh man, your mental state is screwed up. You're not surrounded by anything positive. You're just not thinking about anything good or what else is out there. Too many people who get out of tough situations just want out as soon as they have the chance.

"I always think about that now when I drive through Dudley [Square in Roxbury]. Kids are coming home from after-school programs, and in winter it's dark. Everything is closed except the police station. There are homeless people everywhere. All the cops' cars, fancy SUVs, are parked on the street. Most of the cops are white guys. I'm sure very few people think those cops are there to help them."

As we go back and forth, I concede to Jesse. He has helped me to understand how some forms of white "assistance" to communities of color are patronizing rather than empowering. While I still am involved in work to improve conditions in disadvantaged communities, I like to think that today my work is more nuanced. It is about channeling resources that otherwise would not be accessible to those communities and supporting local leaders, the people Jesse talked about who have the ability to leave but choose to stay, training residents to be advocates for policies that redress historical inequities.

It's also about working with white people to understand how systemic racism works and understand our place in a different way.

When Jesse was in his early teens, we used to argue about whether racism was a problem. Even back then, he took the position that his peers of color had opportunities; they just didn't take advantage of them. Then he was fifteen and tried hailing a cab on a Saturday night with his friends of color. They learned that the only way to get a cab was for Jesse, the white boy, to step out alone. Once the cab stopped and Jesse got his foot in the door, his friends would join him, and it was too late for the cabbie to do anything but give them a ride home. When I remind Jesse of this experience now, he responds, "This makes a case for exposing kids to other worlds. At a young age, it's very important. Unless you do that, it's never going to get any better."

In the final analysis, we are not so very far apart in our thinking, except that, in my mind, the exposure needs to go beyond "other worlds." It needs to include learning about the racially restrictive laws and practices that so many of our country's institutions were built upon. Without this, it is too easy for white people to blame people of color for policies and conditions they did not create and continue to have little power over. And it is too easy for people of color, particularly African Americans, to think that the problems in their lives are strictly of their own personal making. This is not to minimize the need for each of us to take responsibility for our own individual actions. But a deeper dive into the structural barriers perpetuated by our nation's institutions can help us all accept shared responsibility for creating a truly equitable society.

* * *

In December 2004, my second four-year term on the Boston School Committee was ending. Ben and Jesse were both high school graduates, and I was no longer a parent of children in the school system. It was time to move on. I was ready for a break, a return to some semblance of a normal life. I had also convinced Michele, the Burke High School parent who was instrumental in securing the resources for that school to regain accreditation, to apply for the seat I was vacating.

When word got out that I was stepping down, I got a phone call from a *Boston Globe* reporter. He prodded, thinking I was being pushed out for my outspokenness and contrary votes.

No, it was just time to move on.

The article he then wrote called me "the skunk in the school committee garden party." I had no regrets for the role I played. My persistent questions often brought better information into the school system's decision making. My outreach to parents and community groups built bridges and credibility, even if they were fragile at times. My insider support on positions helped grassroots groups be heard, resulting in more responsive policies and structures.

It was time to make room for new leadership and to learn to breathe again.

* * *

As I started to let people know I was writing this book, Todd, the director of a metro Boston leadership program, encouraged me to share my writing with program participants. LeadBoston brought together a diverse group of emerging leaders for a yearlong program that exposed them to different facets of Boston. Todd had first invited me to meet with the group the week they were assigned to visit schools across Boston. Many had never set foot in a Boston public school; others were teachers and administrators within some of these schools. I offered to send a few draft chapters to anyone in the program who agreed to review them and provide feedback.

When we met, the parents in the audience were dismayed at the realization that, fifteen years later, little had changed. White parents still dominated the parent organizations in many Boston Public Schools, despite being a small minority of the school population. Issues of race and entitlement were still rarely discussed, and certainly not in the schools of those parents attending my book discussion. Parenting had become more competitive, even as the children who are given all the advantages showed increasing signs of alienation and distress, in the form of more behavioral problems and an ever-expanding use of psychotropic drugs to manage them.

"But what's wrong with privilege?" one white woman asked me. "You make it sound like a bad thing, but aren't the privileges you describe what every parent would want if they had the chance? If any disadvantaged group is successful at gaining resources for their kids and coming into power in the same way, wouldn't we want them to feel entitled to it?" This set of questions kept me awake at night. Maybe she was right. Was I being self-righteous all along? Too focused on past inequities to see the obvious?

I have come to believe the answer is not either/or. Of course all children should be entitled to effective teachers, a safe and supportive environment, and an education that provides them with basic skills, expands their understanding, and increases their life options. But this does not mean that these need to be obtained at somebody else's expense.

And I'm not convinced that "privilege," defined as having unearned access to most-favored status, is a healthy aspiration. There is a psychic price that comes with this form of privilege, at least in a nominally democratic society. Our nation was founded on a stated belief in fairness and the ability of all people to succeed if they put in the effort. These principles, initially applied only to free white men, were eventually amended to include people of color and women. For those among us who have unearned privilege, a certain level of aggression and denial is required to maintain this most-favored status. Otherwise, the contradictions of our nation's systems would drive us crazy—or spur us to wake up and challenge them.

As long as some people view a high-quality public education as a zero-sum game, in which some children win at the expense of others, it's predictable that they will fight for their own. If we all believed, however, that there should be enough to go around, the fight shifts to a collective effort. We begin to see how getting what we need at somebody else's expense does not, in the long run, serve our interests. It only creates other societal problems for which we all end up paying.

When businesses can't find the educated workforce they need, when undereducated adults work at jobs that don't provide a living wage, and when prison budgets grow larger than education budgets—as is now the case throughout the United States—we all pay the price.

As I complete this book, the United States has unprecedented poverty rates and income gaps between rich and poor. College attendance rates, at their peak in 1975 for whites, blacks, and Latinos, have been steadily slipping ever since. States have cut spending for public education by a total of over $10 billion in 2010 and 2011 alone.

At the same time, federal educational policy is based on punishing those schools that are not succeeding with all students. Funding continues at a tiny dribble of what is needed. This is like cutting off entire communities at the knees and then asking them to dance. And those communities continue to be the poorest communities of black, Latino, and immigrant families.

While the solutions are not simple, complacency is not one of them. We each have an important role to play, no matter how small.

We can reach out to people who are different from us. The simple act of reaching out to my son's schoolmates created bridges across great chasms. Those of us with options can make housing and education decisions that increase the likelihood that we, and our children, will cross paths with people who are different from ourselves.

We can ask questions such as, Why are students of color disproportionately failing in the schools in our community? That simple question opened up a universe of understanding for me. And an important part of that answer came from listening to the perspectives of the students and families who were the subject of my question.

We can educate ourselves about the systemic nature of racism and the history of racial segregation and institutional barriers that have created the inequities we face today. There was so much I never knew until I actively sought out such information. We can vote for state and local budgets that reduce these inequities of opportunity, and we can support elected officials who reflect such values.

As white people, we can "lead from behind." This means supporting those who are less confident or have more obstacles in their lives so that they can more fully participate in decision making in our schools and communities. I found power and wisdom released by the simple act of stopping a parent meeting and asking if anybody who hadn't yet spoken had something to say.

We can raise children to understand that we are only as well off as the larger society in which we live.

And I have no doubt our children will thank us for this.

* * *

No big-city school system in the United States has figured out how to adequately prepare all students for high levels of academic achievement. There is no formula yet developed and tested.

Yet, in the wealthiest nation on earth, it is unconscionable that every school and every classroom do not have adequate supplies and facilities. I will never forget a parent meeting where a father stood up and said, "I come from Haiti, one of the poorest countries on earth. In Haiti, I understand when our classrooms have no books and there is no glass in the windows. But here in America, this is the richest country in the world. How can it be that the schools don't have enough textbooks and the classroom windows are broken?"

We live in the country with the greatest income gap between corporate leaders and the people who work for them. It would take very little off the top to ensure adequate resources to pay teachers a wage that allows them to live secure, middle-class lives. This, in turn, would give us a chance at attracting and retaining a steady pipeline of talented and dedicated new people into the teaching profession.

What concerns me is the way to get to these changes. It is the relationships, the *how* of improving public schools, that we do not pay enough attention to.

On the Boston School Committee, I regularly saw proven policies undermined by the people charged to implement them. People in large institutions get really good at going through the motions necessary to keep their jobs. Who's to blame them, if there has been no process to include them in the decision making, and they fundamentally don't agree that what is being asked of them will produce the desired results?

Public schools reflect our values, hopes, and dreams for the future—for our children, our communities, our country. The reasons our public schools do not succeed with every child are complex but not unsolvable. We can start by taking the time to articulate our shared values, voice our hopes, and create a collective vision within our communities. This is a very different decision-making process than that being used by most school systems in this country, and yet it is the heart of democracy.

The opportunity gap in our schools is about more than money. At its core, it is about the opportunity to participate in the decisions that affect our families, our communities, and our lives.

* * *

I started this final chapter sitting on a porch overlooking the Atlantic Ocean, on Maine's Monhegan Island, one of my favorite retreats. It's a four-hour drive northeast from Boston, followed by a one-hour ferry ride to the island, ten miles out to sea. It was October, and the summer visitors and second-home owners had left for the year. The ferry schedule from the mainland was down to one boat a day out of the tiny fishing village of Port Clyde.

The year-round population on Monhegan Island hovers between forty and sixty, depending on whether you count those who claim this as their permanent residence but quietly depart when the ferry service cuts back to just three trips a week, weather permitting.

The owners of the place where I stay raised three children here. The oldest two were sent to boarding school on the mainland for high school, a common practice for Maine island kids. Their mother tells me what a shock it was for her son, going from a class of two his last year at the Monhegan Island School to a school of hundreds, where he had to share a bedroom with three other boys.

I asked her how many children there were at the Monhegan Island School now.

"Well, let me see: there's Julia and Bobby and…" She lifts a finger with each name she recites. "Five."

Her son couldn't believe how rough the boys were when he went off island to school.

"He had never encountered bullying before and couldn't understand why they were so mean. He ended up dropping out, and still struggles with social skills."

After this experience, she moved to the mainland from September through June for five years so her daughter could attend a regular public high school. Her children, now adults, are adamant that they would never raise their own children on Monhegan Island. It's too isolated, too protected; it leaves children lacking in skills to survive a larger world.

She shared her children's school experiences with me as we stood on the back deck of her house overlooking the harbor, full of lobster boats anchored in a light breeze. In response, I casually mentioned how my kids experienced the other extreme. I don't say it aloud, but I have no doubt that they know how to handle themselves in almost any situation.

As I complete this story, Ben has just turned thirty. After graduating from college, he moved to New York City, where he landed a job doing international human rights work. Contrary to my concerns when he was little that he would use family connections to slide into an easy life, he got this job on his own credentials. During Ben's senior year of college, my sister put him in contact with a friend of hers who was a successful national political operative. After they talked on the phone, her friend remarked to her, "Your nephew has a better Rolodex than I do."

Ben's work has taken him to prisons in Mexico, Darfuri refugee camps in Chad, village-based truth and reconciliation gatherings in Rwanda, and an international meeting of reform-minded police chiefs in Tbilisi. He is now pursuing an Ivy League graduate degree in public affairs.

Jesse started to follow round-the-world sailboat races on the Internet when he was in high school and captain of Boston Latin School's sailing team. By the time he was a junior, he asked one day over dinner, "Do you think Grandpa would be mad if I used the money he gave us for college to buy a sailboat instead?" This money was one more reminder of how family resources, or lack thereof, flow through the generations, continuously enhancing or narrowing life possibilities.

At age twenty, Jesse took the college funds and flew to Brazil to buy a twenty-one-foot racing sailboat that he sailed back to Boston alone. The next year he completed a transatlantic solo race from France to Brazil. He has since leveraged his love of sailing into a career managing and racing very fast sailboats. He was the first American to make it onto the podium of one of the most prestigious France-to Central America sailboat races. His current project is paying him to coskipper a sixty-foot racing sailboat on an almost complete circumnavigation of the world, from Australia to China to South Africa, then on to Brazil, through the Panama Canal and up the west coast of the United States.

What Ben and Jesse were exposed to as a result of John's and my decision to send them to the Boston Public Schools caused plenty of anxiety along the way. But that was the package deal that came with living in the city. I held my breath for many years, wondering if these adult decisions of ours would really benefit our sons in the ways I hoped they would. Now that they are both young adults, I can exhale, knowing the answer is a resounding YES! We have prepared them well to live in this world, wherever they tread.

John eventually became frustrated with the educational constraints of being a classroom teacher. After six years, he launched a program that builds boats with fifth graders in the Boston Public Schools. His program now includes sailing in the Boston Harbor and doing oral histories with people of color in the maritime industry, integrating science, math, and social studies with experiential learning.

Ben's childhood friend Ernesto's first marriage didn't work out. He recently remarried, and I was honored to attend an intimate wedding with mostly family members. I could see how this new relationship has been good for him. He is nurturing a new love for photography and taking college courses. He admits that the classes are too easy, but he doesn't believe he would be taken seriously if he applied to a four-year college without first earning an associate's degree. Ernesto's oldest son, now thirteen, has a mentor from Harvard University, where he has spent a lot of time. Ernesto is doing his best to ensure that he creates a trajectory of wider opportunity for his own children.

Klare, cochair with me of the Trotter Elementary School Parent Council, has continued to work in the philanthropic world of Boston as a tireless advocate for public education, parent and youth organizing, and arts education. She recently moved into a role as special advisor to the superintendent of the Boston Public Schools.

Michele, the parent organizer who filed the civil rights complaint that was instrumental in rescuing the Burke High School, went on to become the first executive director of the Boston Parent Organizing Network. She then was appointed to the seat I left at the end of my second four-year term on the Boston School Committee. Michele is now assistant superintendent for family and student engagement for the Boston Public Schools.

In that role, she has instituted a nationally recognized parent university that trains hundreds of parents every year in how to engage their children's schools and better support student achievement.

Karen, who helped me facilitate two rounds of school committee–sponsored community forums, became the Boston Public Schools' first deputy superintendent for family and community engagement. She is now a lecturer and program director of the Education, Policy and Management Master's Program at Harvard University Graduate School of Education. She recently completed research and coauthored a book on community organizing for school reform.

Liz, the school committee chair during most of my tenure, retired from the school committee at the end of 2008, with the distinction of having been the longest-serving school board chair in Boston history.

The Patrick Gavin Middle School, whose politics club gave me a lesson in budget priorities, was designated for restructuring by the state in 2006 because of chronically low standardized test scores. The school was closed following the 2010–11 school year and was replaced with Boston's first privately run charter school under contract with the Boston Public Schools. The teachers union president was quoted as saying that tapping a private firm to run a public school was an insult to educators employed by the city. The new school had four thousand applicants for sixty staff positions.

The Orchard Gardens K-8 School, after being led by six different principals in its first seven years, now has stable leadership and rising test scores. It was selected in 2012 to take part in the highly competitive national Turnaround Arts program, which provides resources for enhanced art and music programming. In February 2012, a class from Orchard Gardens was invited to recite Martin Luther King Jr.'s "I Have a Dream" speech at the White House.

The Boston Public Schools, after four years as a finalist, won the Broad Prize for Urban Education in 2006. The award as the best urban school district in the nation came with $1 million in college scholarships for the school system's graduates. More recently, Boston's fourth and eighth grade students' gains in math exceeded the national average on the National Assessment of Education Progress. The district's four-year graduation rate for the class of 2009 exceeded 60 percent for the first time since the state began keeping data, while the annual dropout rate for the 2008–09 school year, at 6.4 percent, was the lowest in more than two decades. The school system is frequently cited as a model for urban school district reform.

* * *

The one-room schoolhouse on Monhegan Island, Maine, is about as far as one can get from the Boston Public Schools—if not physically, certainly economically, racially, and psychologically. The former may represent the ultimate protection from the dangers of the world, the latter the riskier proposition. While it is a parent's instinct to protect their children from harm, it is also a parent's responsibility to give their children the skills to make their way in the world.

And it is all of our responsibility, as adults living in a democracy, to ensure that we provide our country's children with the range of opportunities necessary to do so.

Sources Cited

Introduction

Jacoby, Jeff. "Busing's legacy: racial isolation." Boston Globe, *January 7, 1999.*

Population: Race, Hispanic Origin, and Veteran Status. *Boston Redevelopment Authority Special File created from 1970 and 1980 Census of Population and Housing. State Data Center, Massachusetts Institute for Social & Economic Research, University of Massachusetts Amherst.*

Report of the National Advisory Commission on Civil Disorders. (The Kerner Report.) February 29, 1968.

1. "They Need Whites There"

Race: The Power of an Illusion. Produced by Larry Adelman. California Newsreel, 2003.

3. Contact Zones

Fact Sheet. Citywide Educational Coalition, June 1988.

Roberts, Hayley. "Implicit Bias and Social Justice." *Open Society Foundations Blog*, December 18, 2011. http://blog.soros.org/2011/12/implicit-bias-and-social-justice.

Robinson, Ken. *The Element.* New York: Viking, 2009.

We Dream a World: The 2025 Vision for Black Men and Boys. New York: Twenty-First Century Foundation, 2010.

"What Americans Keep Ignoring about Finland's School Success." *Atlantic*, December 29, 2011.

Zernike, Kate. "Studies Point Up Racial Discrimination in Special Education." *New York Times*, March 3, 2001.

7. Lost in the Shuffle

Council of the Great City Schools. "Urban School Superintendents: Characteristics, Tenure, and Salary—Fourth Biennial Survey." *Urban Indicator: A Research Publication* 7, no. 1 (October 2003).

Jerald, Craig D. *Dispelling the Myth Revisited.* The Education Trust, 2001.

Lazar, Kay. "Dorchester principal shares his success." *Boston Herald*, January 10, 1999.

8. On Metal Detectors and Other Priorities

Cohen, Muriel. "More Top Students Turning to Tutors to Keep Their Edge." *Boston Globe*, February 21, 1999.

Funding for Justice: Money, Equity, and the Future of Public Education. Rethinking Schools, 1997.

Kaplan, Fred. "Pentagon gets $1b it has no use for." *Boston Globe*, October 24, 1998.

Left Behind in America: The Nation's Dropout Crisis. Center for Labor Market Studies, Northeastern University, October 2009.

School Finance: Per-Pupil Spending Differences between Selected Inner City and Suburban Schools Varied by Metropolitan Area. GAO-03-234. Report to the Ranking Minority Member, Committee on Ways and Means, House of Representatives. United States General Accounting Office, December 2002.

Warren, Mark R., and Karen L. Mapp. *A Match on Dry Grass: Community Organizing as a Catalyst for School Reform.* New York: Oxford University Press, 2011.

9. Fresh Air

A Class Divided. Directed by William Peters. *PBS: Frontline*, March 26, 1985. http://www.pbs.org/wgbh/pages/frontline/shows/divided.

11. Reflections in the Rearview Mirror

Darling-Hammond, Linda. "Why Is Congress Redlining our Schools?" *Nation*, January 30, 2012.

Young, Colin A. "Roxbury school gets arts boost." *Boston Globe*, April 24, 2012.

Resources

There are many resources available on the topics covered in this book. Below are some I have found instructive and accessible.

Racial Equity in Public Education

Delpit, Lisa. *Other People's Children: Cultural Conflict in the Classroom*. New York: New Press, 1995.

Diversity Matters: Why We Should Create & Sustain Diversity in Schools: A CHHIRJ Policy Brief. Cambridge, MA: Charles Hamilton Houston Institute for Race & Justice at Harvard Law School, 2009.

Lindsey, Randall B., Kikanza Nuri Robins, and Raymond D. Terrell. *Cultural Proficiency: A Manual for School Leaders*. Thousand Oaks, CA: Corwin Press, 2009.

Pollock, Mica, ed. *Everyday Antiracism: Getting Real about Race in School*. New York: New Press, 2008.

Rethinking Schools, www.rethinkingschools.org. This national publisher of educational materials, including a blog, monthly online and print magazine, helps educators and others understand and address inequities in public education, with an emphasis on urban schools and issues of race.

Singleton, Glenn E., and Curtis Linton. *Courageous Conversations about Race: A Field Guide for Achieving Equity in Schools*. Thousand Oaks, CA: Corwin Press, 2006.

Tatum, Beverly Daniel. *"Why Are All the Black Kids Sitting Together in the Cafeteria?": And Other Conversations about Race*. Revised edition. New York: Basic Books, 1999.

Teaching Tolerance, a project of the Southern Poverty Law Center, www.teachingtolerance.org

Organizing for Education Reform

Center for Education Organizing. *Getting Started in Education Organizing: Resources and Strategies*. Annenberg Institute for School Reform, 2012.

Education for Liberation Network, www.edliberation.org

Warren, Mark R., and Karen L. Mapp. *A Match on Dry Grass: Community Organizing as a Catalyst for School Reform*. New York: Oxford University Press, 2011.

White People's Roles in Challenging Racial Inequity

Kivel, Paul. *Uprooting Racism: How White People Can Work for Racial Justice*. Revised edition. Gabriola Island, BC: New Society Publishers, 2002.

McIntosh, Peggy. "White Privilege: Unpacking the Invisible Knapsack." *Peace and Freedom* (July/August 1989).

Warren, Mark R. *Fire in the Heart: How White Activists Embrace Racial Justice*. New York: Oxford University Press, 2010.

History of Integration of the Boston Public Schools

Boston Busing/Desegregation Project for Truth, Learning & Change, www.bbdplearningnetwork.wordpress.com

Kendrick, Stephen, and Paul Kendrick. *Sarah's Long Walk: The Free Blacks of Boston and How Their Struggle for Equality Changed America*. Boston: Beacon Press, 2004.

Lukas, J. Anthony. *Common Ground: A Turbulent Decade in the Lives of Three American Families*. New York: Vintage Books, 1985.

Other Racial Justice Resources

Applied Research Center, www.arc.org. The work of this public policy, educational, and research institute emphasizes issues of race and social change.

Aspen Institute Roundtable on Community Change, www.aspeninstitute.org/policy-work/community-change/racial-equity . The Roundtable's work on Racial Equity includes seminars and many useful publications.

A Class Divided, www.pbs.org/wgbh/pages/frontline/shows/divided. This film and related discussion guide documents an experiment where children, and later adults, are divided based on eye color and treated based on different stereotypes. Participant reactions show how negative stereotypes influence behavior to a startling degree.

Community Change, Inc, www.communitychangeinc.org. This Boston-based antiracist education and organizing group runs a Resource Center with online links to a wealth of racial justice resources, including publications, websites, webinars, and other like-minded organizations.

Kirwan Institute for the Study of Race and Ethnicity, www.kirwaninstitute.org. The Institute's research and partnerships have been significant in reframing racial and ethnic disparities around understanding opportunity gaps. They also host an informative blog, www.race-talk.org.

The People's Institute for Survival and Beyond, www.pisab.org. This national organization offers workshops, technical assistance, and consultation to individuals, communities, organizations, and institutions. Workshops "utilize a systemic approach that emphasizes learning from history, developing leadership, maintaining accountability to communities, creating networks, undoing internalized racial oppression and understanding the role of organizational gate keeping as a mechanism for perpetuating racism."

Race: The Power of an Illusion, www.pbs.org/race. This three-part documentary film with accompanying viewer's guide dismantles common myths and misconceptions about race, scrutinizes assumptions, and exposes the underlying social, economic, and political conditions that have disproportionately channeled advantages and opportunities to white people in the United States.

Racism Review, www.racismreview.com/blog/

Racial Equity Tools, www.racialequitytools.org

Index

About the Author

 SUSAN NAIMARK is a consultant and trainer who works with public school parents, grassroots groups, and nonprofit and public agencies to create responsive community institutions. She was a founder of the Boston Parent Organizing Network, a member of the school board for the city of Boston, and has served in leadership roles with several national nonprofit community development organizations. Susan's home since 1977 has been the Boston neighborhood of Jamaica Plain, where she and her husband raised two now-adult sons.